THE CAUSES OF THE
1929 STOCK MARKET CRASH

Recent Titles in
Contributions in Economics and Economic History

The Causes of the 1929 Stock Market Crash

A Speculative Orgy or a New Era?

Harold Bierman, Jr.

Contributions in Economics and
Economic History, Number 195

GREENWOOD PRESS
Westport, Connecticut • London

Library of Congress Cataloging-in-Publication Data

Bierman, Harold.
    The causes of the 1929 stock market crash : a speculative orgy or
a new era? / Harold Bierman, Jr.
        p.   cm.—(Contributions in economics and economic history,
ISSN 0084–9235 ; no. 195)
    Includes bibliographical references and index.
    ISBN 0–313–30629–X (alk. paper)
    1. Depressions—1929—United States.   2. Stock exchanges—United
States—History—20th century.   3. Wall Street—History—20th
century.   I. Title.   II. Series.
    HB3717   1929.B388   1998
    338.5'4'097309043—DC21   97–32007

British Library Cataloguing in Publication Data is available.

Copyright © 1998 by Harold Bierman, Jr.

Library of Congress Catalog Card Number: 97–32007
ISBN: 0–313–30629–X
ISSN: 0084–9235

First published in 1998

Greenwood Press, 88 Post Road West, Westport, CT 06881
An imprint of Greenwood Publishing Group, Inc.

Printed in the United States of America

The paper used in this book complies with the
Permanent Paper Standard issued by the National
Information Standards Organization (Z39.48–1984).

10 9 8 7 6 5 4 3 2 1

Contents

Tables

Preface

In 1991 I wrote a book titled *The Great Myths of 1929 and the Lessons to Be Learned.* There were seven myths about 1929 that I discussed and refuted. The myth that is most relevant to this book is (*The Great Myths*, p. 14) "Stocks were obviously overpriced (the evidence suggests stocks were reasonably priced)."

The stock market, in general, was not unreasonably priced, but I do want to refine my conclusion based on additional research. While I still think stocks were not obviously overpriced in general, there was one sector of the market, public utilities, that can be shown to be overpriced, and two sectors, the investment trusts and banks, that may have been overpriced.

This book is an attempt to define the causes of the 1929 stock market crash. In 1991 I could refute the myths, but I could not explain the crash. Now I have reasonable explanations. There were several factors that combined in October 1929 to bring it about.

It is important that the causes be properly understood, because the 1929 stock market was not that much different than the market today or different than the market could be at any time in the future.

OTHER READINGS

There have been many books written about 1929 and the great crash. On the optimistic end of the spectrum are Fisher (1930),

Lawrence (1929), and Bierman (1991). Schwed (1940) wrote the humorous classic *Where Are the Customers' Yachts?*

Hoover's autobiography (1952) is important for understanding the war the federal government was waging against speculators. Galbraith (1961) provides color and is very readable. In the same vein are Thomas and Morgan-Witts (1979) and Schachtman (1979).

Wigmore (1985) is an extremely valuable source of data and serious descriptions of events.

McDonald (1962) tells the Insull story and Pecora (1939) the story of the 1933 Congressional Hearings, especially the Mitchell and Wiggin affairs. Jones and Lowe (1935) seek out market manipulation.

Kindleberger (1978) places the 1929 crash in the historical frame of other "Manias and Panics."

REWRITING HISTORY

There are several conclusions reached in this book that are contrary to the conventional historical record. There is need for a revision of history on these aspects of 1929. They include the following:

1. The general level of the stock market was not too high in 1929 if we use financial fundamentals to evaluate stocks.

2. The 1929 business conditions were sound, and there was reason for optimism. There was no general news to trigger the crash.

3. Irving Fisher did not manage the Yale endowment so that it was highly speculative in 1929.

4. The Hatry Affair was exotic but not likely to have been a significant factor in the U.S. market crash.

5. There is no reason to think that illegal acts of stock market manipulation caused the boom or the crash.

6. Charles E. Mitchell, chairman of National City Bank, deserves much fairer treatment by historians.

7. Albert H. Wiggin, president of Chase, is more suspect than Mitchell—not because of his 1929 dealings with Chase stock but rather his dealings with BMT stock, which were clearly inappropriate. But these BMT stock transactions were done in 1932, thus not highly relevant for a 1929 crash study.

8. Sam Insull should have been an American hero, but he used too much debt in a period that turned into the 1930 depression. He deserves much better from history because of his real accomplishments. He was not convicted of any crimes. He was destroyed by the press and the federal government.

Acknowledgments

This book was written during a study leave spent at the Judge Institute of Management, University of Cambridge. The leave and the research were financed by the Arthur Andersen Foundation and Cornell's Johnson Graduate School of Management. Richard Barker, Sandra Dawson, Gishan Dissanaike, Geoff Meeks, Christopher Pratt, and Geoff Wittington all facilitated my visit and made it a very pleasant experience. At Cornell, Sheri Hastings kept my faxes flowing. Lynn Brown of the Johnson School library offered substantive assistance.

The copyeditor for Greenwood Publishing, Marlowe Bergendoff, did an outstanding job and I thank her.

Above all I want to thank the people at the University of Cambridge Library, especially Ann Toseland; Ann kept me supplied with film of the newspapers of 1929 to 1950, and did not complain of my repetitive requests. While the others are unnamed by me (unfortunately), their helpfulness is well remembered.

I also want to thank Burton Malkiel who offered a friendly intellectual challenge that led to this, my second, excursion into the past.

THE CAUSES OF THE
1929 STOCK MARKET CRASH

CHAPTER 1

Was the Stock Market Too High?

"However, contemporary and historical accounts have failed to find
even a smoking gun, let alone a culprit."

Rappoport and White (1993, p. 570)

On Black Thursday, October 24, 1929, the stock market (New York
Stock Exchange) fell 34 points, a 9 percent drop for the day. The
trading volume was approximately three times the normal daily volume for the first nine months of the year. There was a selling panic.
But the series of events leading to the crash actually started before
that date.

It is important that we more fully understand the causes of the
1929 stock market crash and correct some of the widely held misconceptions. If stock prices were too high because of speculative
buying, and the crash was inevitable, then the lesson to be preached
is simple, if not easily executed. One should not invest in stocks if
stock prices are too high. The conventional wisdom is that speculation was the cause of stock prices being too high. Thus Malkiel
(1996) writes (p. 51) about a speculative boom:

Perhaps the best summary of the debacle was given by *Variety*,
the show-business weekly, which headlined the story, "Wall
Street Lays an Egg." The speculative boom was dead and bil-

lions of dollars of share values—as well as the dreams of millions—were wiped out.

Laying the blame for the "boom" on speculators was even more common in 1929. Thus immediately upon learning of the crash of October 24 John Maynard Keynes wrote in the *New York Evening Post* (October 25, 1929): "The extraordinary speculation on Wall Street in past months has driven up the rate of interest to an unprecedented level" (Moggridge, 1981, p. 2 of Vol. xx). And the *Economist*, when stock prices reached their low for the year, repeated the theme that the U.S. stock market had been too high (November 2, 1929, p. 806): "There is warrant for hoping that the deflation of the exaggerated balloon of American stock values will be for the good of the world."

The key phrases in the above quotations are "exaggerated balloon of American stock values" and "extraordinary speculation on Wall Street." The common viewpoint was that the United States stock market was too high.

But if the conventional view of history is not correct and if U.S. stocks were not universally too high, then what did cause the great crash? The stock market index hit a high of 386 in September 1929, and by November it had dropped to 230, a drop of 40 percent. By the time the crash was completed in 1932—and thanks to the oncoming of the real economic depression—stocks had lost in excess of 70 percent of their value. The results of the crash were devastating to individuals and to nations. The crash helped bring on the depression of the thirties and the depression helped to extend the period of low stock prices, thus "proving" that the prices had been too high. This book will review a small set of possible causes of the crash and will reach specific conclusions that might cast some light on the causes of this important event. The lessons for investors and students of history are important. While I will not prove that I know the exact specific causes of the crash, I will present some reasonable evidence that supports the hypotheses.

Table 1.1
Dow-Jones Industrials Index,* Average of the Highs and Lows

	Index
1922	91.0
1923	95.6
1924	104.4
1925	137.2
1926	150.9
1927	177.6
1928	245.6
1929	290.0
1930	225.8
1931	134.1
1932	79.4

*1922–1929 measures are from the Stock Market Study, U.S. Senate, 1955, pp. 40, 49, 110, and 111.

1930–1932 average of the lows and highs for the years, Wigmore, 1985, pp. 637–39.

THE 1929 MARKET

Table 1.1 shows the average of the highs and lows of the Dow Jones Industrial Stock Index for 1922 to 1932.

Using the information of Table 1.1, from 1922 to 1929 stocks rose in value by 218.7 percent. This is equivalent to an 18 percent annual growth rate in value for the seven years. From 245.6 of 1928 to the high of 386 in 1929 was a 57 percent growth, but using the 290.0 measure for 1929 the increase for 1929 was only 15 percent. From 1929 to 1932 stocks lost 73 percent of their value (different indices measured at different times would give different measures of the increases and decreases). The price increases were large but not beyond comprehension. The price decreases taken to 1932 were consistent with the fact that by 1932 there was a worldwide depression, and stock price expectations were not optimistic.

If we take the 386 high of September and the 1929 year-end value of 248.48, the market lost 36 percent of its value during that four-month period. Galbraith (1961, p. 29) apparently would have had no difficulty forecasting the crash: "On the first of January of 1929 as a matter of probability, it was most likely that the boom would end before the year was out." Paul A. Samuelson (1979, p. 9) on the other hand admits that "playing as I often do the experiment of studying price profiles with their dates concealed, I discovered that I would have been caught by the 1929 debacle."

Most of us, if we held stock in September 1929, would not have sold early in October. In fact, if I had liquidity, I would have purchased stocks after the major break on Black Thursday, October 24. For the next ten years, I would have been sorry since Black Thursday was not the end of the decline.

The 1929 stock market, for many reasons, was like a large boulder on the top of a hill. Given enough pushes to get it started, the boulder will roll down the hill, accelerating as it goes. We want to consider why the market was in such a sensitive position and what factors acted to start its downward fall. We will find that there were many contributing factors leading up to the crash. Each of them is small taken individually, but together they helped create the right situation for the debacle.

Even those observers who thought the market was too high were not pleased with the severity of the crash. Thus Keynes (Moggridge 1981, p. 1 and 1992, p. 480) in a letter to his wife Lydia (October 25, 1929) wrote, "Wall Street *did* have a go yesterday. . . . The biggest crash ever recorded. . . . I have been in a thoroughly financial and disgusting state of mind all day." Before the event had played out, many others would share Keynes's despondency.

There is evidence that the stone on the hill is an apt description of the market in 1929. In a recent study Rappoport and White (1994) treat brokers' loans as options written by the lender and bought by the borrowers. They conclude (p. 271), "The sharp rise in implied volatility coincident with the stock-market boom suggests the fear of a crash." This conclusion that there was fear of a market crash is easily acceptable given the statements and positions of the Federal Reserve Board and the United States Senate to be described later in this book.

One position is that the stock market was too high, thus a crash was inevitable. We cannot prove that the stock market was reasonably priced at the end of September 1929, but reasons will be given for the level of prices. It is also difficult to prove that the market was too high.

There are two basic but naive and incorrect methods of "proving" the stock market was too high in September–October 1929, using only stock prices. One is to compare the stock market prices for some prior period, say 1925, and September 1929. The stock price increases for this time period are impressive. Balke and Gordon (1986) show a 155 percent increase (the third quarter 1929 stock prices are 2.55 times as large as the 1925 prices). During the first nine months of 1929 the increase was 15 percent. The market did go up dramatically from 1925 to October 1929.

The second method of "proving" the market was too high is to compare the September 1929 prices with those in November 1929 or, more impressively, with prices in 1932. In 1932 prices were 32 percent of the year-end 1929 prices. They went down. Malkiel (1996, p. 50) uses the following stock prices (Table 1.2) to illustrate the excessive heights that stocks reached in September 1929.

Obviously, either the September prices are too high or the November prices are too low, or the world changed. But just comparing stock prices merely shows that changes took place. Is there a plausible explanation for the September 3, 1929, prices? We will consider the price earnings ratios of the above companies.

In evaluating the P/E's of firms in 1929 it is useful to estimate the costs of capital. Long-term debt was yielding approximately 5 percent and preferred stock 6 percent. Dividend yield on the average stock was 3.19 percent in August and the dividend payout rate was .64. For comparison, U.S. Treasuries in August of 1929 yielded 3.7 percent.

With a retention rate of $b = .36$ and a return on new investment

Table 1.2
Selected Stock Prices in 1929

	High Price September 3, 1929	Low Price November 12, 1929
American Telephone & Telegraph	304	197¼
Bethlehem Steel	140⅜	78¼
General Electric	393¼	168⅛
Montgomery Ward	137⅞	49¼
National Cash Register	127½	59
Radio Corporation of America	101	28

of r = .14, the expected growth rate is g = rb = .14(.36) = .05. The cost of equity is approximately 8.2 percent. With these assumptions and facts, a P/E of 20 is justified for the average firm.

$$\frac{P}{E} = \frac{(1-b)}{k-g} = \frac{.64}{.082 - .05} = 20$$

With .06 growth rate a P/E of 29 would be justified.

Adding growth from the use of debt and from issuing new equity capital, a larger P/E than 20 would be justified. There is a wide range of calculations of actual average P/E's for 1929. One estimate in Bierman (1991, p. 59, based on statistics from Moody's) is an average P/E of 16.3, which is low compared to the 20 computed above. Wigmore (1985, p. 572) found a P/E of 29.8 using the high stock prices and 12.4 using the low prices of 1929. These P/E's are based on the data of 135 companies. Irvin Fisher estimated the P/E ratio to be 13 for the market as of August 1929 (*Commercial and Financial Chronicle*, October 26, 1929).

The use of different companies and data from different times

Table 1.3
Price Earning Ratios for the Corporations of Table 1.2

	Using the High Price for 1929	Using the Low Price for 1929
American Telephone & Telegraph	20	13
Bethlehem Steel	13	7
General Electric	43	18
Montgomery Ward	60	16
National Cash Register	28	11
Radio Corporation of America (RCA)	73	17

results in different measures of the P/E ratio in 1929, but the range of estimates seems to be from 12.4 to 29.8 with 16.3 being a reasonable estimate.

Let us consider (Table 1.3) the price-earnings ratios of the same six companies that were included by Malkiel using the high and low prices of 1929 (numbers from Wigmore, 1985, pp. 34–87).

Using the low 1929 prices for all the stocks we have very reasonable P/E ratios ranging from 7 to 18. If anything, given the low cost of equity and high expected growth rate, these P/E's are too low. Using the high prices in the numerators the ratios are somewhat high, especially RCA with an indicated P/E of 73.

The *Wall Street Journal* on October 9 (p. 17) had an article with the heading "Rails Sell 11.9 Times Earnings." This multiple was before the October 24 crash, but it reflected the stock price decreases of September and the first week of October. The P/E measure was for twenty-seven dividend paying railroads. During October the Dow Jones railroad index dropped from 173 to 159, a drop of only 8.1 percent. Railroads were not a bubble on October 1.

On October 22 the *Journal* (p. 3) reported "Utilities Sell at 24 Times Net." The net was for the twelve months ending June 30 and multiple was for twenty representative companies (six were below 20 times earnings). At the end of July they had been selling for 35 times earnings. A day later the *Journal* (p. 1) reported that aviation issues were selling at 12 times net after their market value was reduced 56 percent (the P/E had been 23). The earnings used were the estimated 1929 earnings. The above P/E's were all before Black Thursday.

RCA

Was there any rational explanation for RCA's stock price of $101 on September 3, 1929 (and shown by Malkiel, 1996)? Galbraith (1961, p. 17) called RCA "the speculation symbol of the time." Consider the following measures of earnings per share for RCA for the years 1925, 1927, and 1928.

RCA Earnings Per Share (Before the 5-to-1 Split)	
1925	$ 1.32
1927	6.15
1928	15.98 (3.20 after the stock split)

How much would you pay per share on January 1, 1929, for RCA based on the above earnings record? Moody's gave the firm's preferred stock an A rating. Newspapers carried articles concerning RCA's new products and exciting research efforts. With earnings growing at well over 100 percent per year, it would be easy to conclude that RCA stock was undervalued at $101 (after a five-to-one split). A price of $505 (before the split) is 32 times the $15.98 earnings for 1928. This is high but is not a foolish multiple of earnings given the firm's extraordinary earnings growth of the past four years.

When the crash came it hit RCA very hard. Crashes always hit high growth companies the hardest if the market loses its optimism. The price for RCA stock on November 12, 1929, was $28 down from $101. The 1929 closing price was $44. In 1929 RCA only earned $1.58 per share (down from $3.20). Common stock earnings were said to be depressed by the amount of preferred dividends and interest expenses associated with the acquisition of Victor Talking Machine Company, but the market was not buying the explanation. Consistent with good finance theory, a decrease in the expected growth rate from over 100 percent per year to a decline in earnings resulted in a sharp price decline. But this does not mean that the $101 stock price in September was merely the result of speculative activity. The 1925 to 1928 earnings record was justification for a stock price of this magnitude.

RCA had increased from $32 in 1926 to a high of $420 in 1928. The $420 is more than 13 times as large as the stock's 1926 low. But considering that the earnings were $15.98 per share in 1928, the $420 price is only 26 times earnings. The stock at $420 was not obviously overpriced. The stock continued its increase in 1929, increasing to $505 before the crash. RCA reached a 1929 low (after the five-to-one split) of $28 on November 13, 1929.

RCA attracted a lot of attention from professional investors. In 1929 a pool was formed by M. J. Meehan and Company. The objective of a pool was to buy a company's stock, drive the price up, and then sell before the stock went back down. The pool started buying on March 9, 1929, at a price of $93 and terminated its operations by March 30. During the period of the pool's operations the stock rose to $109.75 and fell as low as $80. The pool made gains of approximately $5 million.

It operated during a period of rising stock prices and made money (it was long in RCA's stock). Newspapers carried articles during the period of the pool's operations that were optimistic about RCA's future. The $15.98 of income for 1928 was compared to the $6.15 income per share for 1927. The pool might have planted some of the bullish stories, but there is no evidence that it did. Conventional wisdom (e.g., Galbraith, 1961, p. 84) was that the pools "manipulated operations." It is not clear that the pool type of activity could significantly affect the market. The buying might cause the price to increase, but the subsequent selling would cause it to decrease. In a talk given to the Bond Club of Washington, D.C., on Friday, October 18, 1929, William P. Hamilton, editor of the *Wall Street Journal*, said that widespread interest in the stock market makes any general manipulation impossible (*Wall Street Journal*, October 19, 1929).

We will consider the price of one other industrial firm. A communication dated October 29 (*Economist*, November 9, 1929, p. 826) gave U.S. Steel's earnings for the third quarter of 1929 to be $51,575,000, up by $21,000,000 over the previous year. The nine-month earnings were $15.80 with $20 per share forecasted for the year (the forecast was low). U.S. Steel's November 7 price was $174 (a P/E of 8.7 using 1929 projected earnings). The high for the year was $261¾ (a P/E of 13). The $261¾ might be too high a price, but an investor would not have to be a "fool" or a "speculator" to buy.

On Sunday, October 13, the *Times* (p. 7) reported that Professor C. A. Dice of Ohio State, an economist, had declared, "Stock Prices Will Stay at High Level for Years to Come." He gave the following justifications (p. 7): "the great economic developments in wealth, in efficiency of production and transportation, in cheapness and adequacy of distribution, in invention and engineering and in public good-will and confidence." He concluded "The day of the small investor is here." Dice was an advocate for the "new era."

Consider the following information regarding performance of U.S. corporations that was readily available in 1929:

1. In the first nine months of 1929, 1,436 firms announced increased dividends (*Forbes*, October 15, 1925, p. 95). In 1928 only 955 announced an increase.

2. In the first nine months, cash dividends were $3.1 billion, up from $2.4 billion in 1928 (a 29 percent increase).

3. In September 1929 dividends were $399 million compared to $278 million in 1928, an increase of 44 percent.

4. The dividend payout was 64 percent in September 1929

compared to 75 percent for September 1928, reflecting increased earnings.

5. Earnings compiled for 650 firms showed a 24.4 percent increase compared to 1928 for the first six months (*National City Bank of New York Newsletter*, August 1929). The earnings for the third quarter for 638 firms was 14.1 percent larger than for 1928. For the first nine months of 1929 the earnings of the 638 firms had increased 20.3 percent compared to 1928 (November 1929, p. 154). The March 1930 issue showed that for 1,509 firms, annual earnings had increased by 13.5 percent for 1929 compared to 1928.

It is not difficult to see why the market was using high expectations of earnings growth. With reasonable (for the time period) estimates of growth, most of the industrial stock prices for September 1929 can be justified with a dividend growth valuation model.

One point of weakness in the market was the low stock dividend yields, especially dividend yields compared to bond yields or to the interest cost of buying stock on margin. For the year 1929 the stock yield was 3.82 percent (*Stock Market Study*, U.S. Senate Hearings, 1955), but as of August 1929 the dividend yield of Moody's 125 industrial was only 3.19 percent (*Stock Market Study*, 1955). Bond yields of 5 percent were normal and preferred stock frequently yielded 6 percent (*Stock Market Study*, 1955, reported bond yields to be 4.73 percent in 1929 for Moody's Aaa corporate bonds). Thus there was a net cash opportunity cost as well as higher risk associated with holding stock. Also, since the borrowing cost associated with carrying stock on margin was equal to or exceeded 5 percent, there was a net cash outlay associated with margin buying. The stock prices had to go up for the investor to feel comfortable. As long as stock prices were increasing at 18 percent per year, the call money financing margin stock purchases at a cost of less than 6 percent was cheap.

THE REAL ECONOMY

The 1920s were a period of real growth and prosperity. Real income rose 10.5 percent per year from 1921 to 1923 and 3.4 percent from 1923 to 1929. The gross national product (GNP) increased in real terms from 296.22 in 1928 to 315.69 in 1929 (Balke and Gordon, 1986, p. 782). The year 1929 was the best year ever for the U.S. economy. The *Federal Reserve Bulletin* showed production at 119 in July; in August it increased to 121, and in September to 123. In October it dropped to 120 but this level of production was still higher than July's level.

There was a widespread feeling that real business activity was in good shape. For example, consider the following from the *Economist*, October 5, 1929 (p. 616):

Meanwhile, business news continues rather good, with exceptionally high rate of production during the summer months. . . . Excellent autumn and holiday trade is anticipated.

During the period 1919–1929 total factor productivity increased at an annual rate of 5.3 percent for the manufacturing sector. This was twice the rate for the entire period studied (the last year studied was 1953 [Kendrick, 1961]). Farming, mining, transportation, communications, and public utilities all did well. Across all industries the period 1919–1929 was the period of most productivity improvement. The *Federal Reserve Bulletin* (1930, p. 494) showed total industrial production at 83 in 1919 and 118 in 1929 (the maximum was 125 in May and June). This was an annual growth rate of 3.6 percent.

There were warning signs, not necessarily observed in October 1929, that real economic activity was slowing. Steel output in September was 416,000 tons below August, and "automobile production decline[d] 82,000 cars practically to level of 1928." These observations were from the *New York Times*, December 31, 1929 (p. 30). They were not likely to be widely known in October. Balancing these belated negative reports were two page-one headlines in October from the *Wall Street Journal* (October 2): "Steel Activity in Sharp Rise" and (October 7) "Motor Output Above Normal." The majority of the economic news reports in October were very favorable.

On October 4 the *Wall Street Journal* (p. 1) had a major headline: "Best September in Typewriters." The article went on to say that sales of typewriters were regarded as a reliable index of business activity, thus there was little chance of a recession.

All of the following measures for September–October 1929 were above the 1923–1926 index measure of 100:

total production

manufacture

building contracts awarded

factory employment

factory payrolls

freight car loadings

Commodity prices were less than 100 and the prices of farm products were at 105.

The business news during the summer and fall of 1929 was very good. On May 24, the *Magazine of Wall Street* carried an article describing the expansion possibilities for electricity in rural areas. The October 1, 1929 issue of *Forbes* described record-breaking rail earnings. The June 15 issue of the *Magazine of Wall Street* stated, "Business so far this year has astonished even the perennial optimists."

When the stock market price break came on Thursday, October 24, the *Economist* (p. 805) observed, "The final collapse of the Wall Street Boom . . . has confounded optimists and pessimists alike." And an important point that is frequently ignored (p. 824): "The share boom of 1926–29 originated in a period of industrial prosperity which has never been surpassed in the world's history." Thus the business news immediately prior to October 24 was extremely positive (except for the regulatory news applicable to the utility sector). As the *Economist* states, it was a period of industrial prosperity that had never been surpassed. Of course, stock prices went up. They went up, not because of speculators, but primarily because of economic facts. If this had not been true, the speculators would have sold the market (or more exactly its components) short and put an end to the boom long before October 24, 1929.

Stephen Cecchetti (1992, p. 576) writes, "We will never know exactly what caused the stock market to fall by nearly 30 percent in late October 1929." He is correct, but there is more to be learned. He also states, "First, there was no reason to believe *a priori* that stock prices were too high before the crash." He identifies (p. 574) as causes the "Federal Reserve behavior, together with the public statements of numerous government officials." The research conducted for this book allows us to expand on these thoughts.

FISHER AND YALE UNIVERSITY

A commonly told tale is that Irving Fisher was the primary advisor to Yale's investment committee in 1929 and that his advice (invest in common stock) was followed with disastrous results. It would actually appear that Yale University in 1929, like universities today, was not inclined to follow completely the advice of its world renowned economist. The investment committee tempered the extreme recommendation, if an extreme recommendation was given by Fisher.

On October 11, 1929, the *New York Times* (p. 16) reported that Yale University's investments totaled $67,695,600. Public utilities represented 35 percent of the total stock investments and railroads 16 percent. The stocks represented 33 percent of the total ($22,339,548). Bonds were 63 percent in 1919 and in 1929 were 38 percent of the total. These changes were noted in a *Times* editorial (October 12, p. 18) but no conclusion was reached by the editor. The stories that were told in academia regarding Irving Fisher and the destruction of Yale's endowment were considerably exaggerated. The 33 percent proportion of the portfolio invested in stocks was a modest amount, and the stocks purchased (51 percent in utilities and railroads) were an attempt to be conservative.

Yale's largest stock holdings (*Wall Street Journal*, October 11, p. 10) were:

American Telephone & Telegraph

Alleghany Corp. Preferred

Union Carbide & Carbon

U.S. Steel Preferred

Union Pacific

Standard Oil (NJ)

Standard Oil Co. of California

Income from investments covered 58 percent of Yale's expenses, and tuition and fees covered 30 percent.

STOCKS AT SEA

On October 1, 1929, the *Wall Street Journal* (p. 15) had an advertisement by M. J. Meehan & Co. announcing a branch office aboard the S. S. Bremen. The office offered "Complete brokerage services on securities." The firm also had offices on the S. S. Berengaria and S. S. Leviathan. The advertisement is typical of the "excesses" that led observers to conclude that Wall Street was the home of speculators and gamblers. On the other hand, one must admit luxury liners were sensible places to locate brokerage offices.

A RESEARCH STUDY

A relatively recent research study by G. J. Santoni concludes that the 1929 and 1987 crashes were not the result of speculative bubbles (Santoni, 1987, p. 28): "The paper provides evidence contrary to the notion that the crashes were the result of bursting speculative bubbles." Rather than a speculative bubble, "the data suggest that the stock prices followed a random walk," and finally (p. 27) "the evidence on the behavior of stock prices (as characterized by the Dow Index) is not consistent with the notion that stock prices were driven by self-feeding speculative bubbles during the 1920's and 1980's."

This conclusion is consistent with Bierman (1991), but in this book we are focusing on the possibility of market segments having inflated prices, rather than evaluating the level of the market as a whole.

A CATALOGUE OF NINE CAUSES

Consider the nine "suspects" that may or may not have caused the crash. The identified causes include:

1. the stock market was too high in September 1929 (values did not justify the prices) because of excessive speculation and the crash was inevitable;

2. a real downturn in business activity;

3. the Hatry affair in England and the subsequent raising of interest rates in London, and liquidation of English investments in the United States;

4. actions of the Federal Reserve Board;

5. the message being sounded by the media and by important governmental figures on both sides of the Atlantic that the U.S. stock was too high and that there was a "war" against the speculators;

6. excessive buying on margin and excessive buying of investment trusts; relative returns and costs of buying on margin;

7. excessive leverage when the debt of operating utilities, holding companies, investment trusts, and margin buying are all considered;

8. the setback in the public utility market arising from an

adverse decision for utilities in Massachusetts combined with an aggressively priced utility market segment;

9. an overreaction by the market.

The first two items were covered in this chapter and rejected as primary causes, though segments of the market were probably too high. We shall analyze each of the remaining causes and conclude that the combination of the last four factors triggered the crash and that the Hatry collapse and the actions of the Federal Reserve Board contributed to it. Unfortunately, there will be no smoking gun, but there is considerable persuasive evidence.

CONCLUSIONS

Based on the arguments offered in this chapter, I conclude that overall stock market was not obviously excessively high in September 1929 and the business outlook was favorable. Thus the October crash did not occur because the market was too high. However, at least one section of the market (public utilities) was too high and too levered, and the stage was set for the selling panic by the press and the governmental officials repeatedly speaking of an orgy of speculation.

CHAPTER 2

The Hatry Case and the 1929 Stock Market Crash

Most authors studying the 1929 stock market crash list the Hatry case as a major contributing factor. Kindleberger (1978, p. 92) in his classic book states, "He was caught using fraudulent collateral in an attempt to borrow £8 million to buy United Steel, and his failure led to a tightening of the British money market, withdrawal of call loans from the New York market, a topping out of the stock market, and the October crash."

The Hatry case makes the financial news starting on September 20, 1929, but we will begin the story in December 1926. Clarence Hatry was the prime mover of a mini-conglomerate engaged in, among other things, photography equipment, industrial machinery, retailing, and light iron goods. In December 1926 he took a major step towards disaster when he founded Corporation and General Securities, Ltd., a company that issued new financial securities. It innovated in two ways. One was by reducing the investment banker's spread, thus reducing the profit opportunities of its competitors. Secondly, it advertised and sold its securities to small investors. In a manner similar to Drexel Burnham fifty years later, it broadened the capital market, making it accessible to less than investment-grade corporations, municipalities, and other entities that needed capital but had previously been shut out or charged relatively large amounts to raise capital. The City (the British financial center) was upset by this brash newcomer who did not follow the traditional ways. The *Economist* (September 28, 1929) stated that from 1927 to mid-1929 the firm had successfully handled fifteen issues for English corporations as well as issues for cities and colonies.

By January 1929 Hatry had decided that a merger of steel companies would result in increased efficiency. He had already successfully joined together several small iron companies. In May 1929 he was ready to execute his plan. The first targeted steel company was United Steel Corporation which was itself a joining together of smaller steel companies and was in financial difficulty with too much debt. In May, Hatry's main firm, Austin Friars Trust, Ltd., signed a contract committing it to buy the stock and debentures of United Steel Corporation, Ltd. United Steel had forty thousand different security holders. The securities being purchased had been issued to these investors at £14 million, but it was obvious to all in May 1929 that this was an inflated value. Austin Friars was to pay the forty thousand investors £5 million and in addition was to pay the firm's bank debt of £3 million. The £8 million payment for United Steel was due in June 1929. Private bankers had informally agreed to supply a temporary loan to accomplish the acquisition.

Unfortunately for Hatry, May 1929 marked the beginning of a general depression in England as the result of a tight money policy. This hurt the cash flow of Hatry's diverse firms. Secondly, the labor party assumed office, weakening business confidence and making it difficult for a marginal entity to borrow. The private bankers walked away from Hatry's deal. Obviously, Hatry did not have a firm commitment from the private bankers.

By the middle of June Austin Friars had paid £3 million of the purchase price. Hatry stated (see Crisp, p. 56) that the firm had firm contracts to borrow £4.7 million, thus Hatry needed to borrow less than £300,000 for three or four days. (Austin Friars was shortly to receive an influx of cash.) The City was aware of Hatry's financing problems and offered no help. They remembered the slicing of margins and other competitive actions by Hatry's investment banking firm. Hatry had already used his personal wealth to support the stock prices of his firms. During Hatry's trial a former solicitor to Hatry, under cross-examination, said that Hatry "had used a personal fortune of £750,000 to meet the liabilities of the Commercial Corporation of London" (*Economist*, January 25, 1930, p. 169). This was in connection with a different financial difficulty of an earlier time period.

To help Austin Friars complete its purchase, Corporate and General Securities made a loan to Austin. It obtained the funds by issuing scrip certificates. Hatry was in effective charge of both firms.

When Corporate and General Securities raised capital by issuing another entity's securities, it first issued its own temporary scrip certificates (denominated £50 and up) to the buyers. These certificates were then exchanged by the buyers for the actual security being issued. An excess of scrip certificates was always on hand so that deals were not delayed by their absence or the absence of the actual securities being issued.

To finance the loan to Austin Friar, Corporate and General Securities borrowed from banks and other firms using the extra scrip as collateral for the loans. The funds raised were supposed to be used to repay earlier loans of Corporate and General Securities (keeping the amount of outstanding scrip constant), but since the loans were not repaid—the money being given to Austin Friars—outstanding scrip exceeded the amount of the underlying securities, and the collateral of the loans was worthless.

Hatry was convicted and sentenced for forgery and conspiracy, but it was later recognized that while there was a crime, it was not forgery. The scrip that was used was of the same vintage as the scrip that was legally used in association with the issue of new securities. The use of the scrip was not forgery.

All agreed (Crisp, p. 6) that "there were serious irregularities." The court decided there were serious crimes. Crisp states regarding Hatry (pp. 4–5), "He is a man of high quality and notable achievement, who was caught in a world depression and hoped, by taking risk, to win through, not for himself, but for his enterprises."

Obviously, Hatry would benefit if his enterprises prospered. Crisp merely meant that the cash from the loans did not flow directly into Hatry's pockets.

Crisp points out that the Hatry case made headlines on September 20, 1929. But there were no obvious market repercussions in either New York or London. The losses in the London market took place after the Wall Street break in late October, not because of Hatry. However, in September three brokerage firms in England failed as a direct result of the Hatry collapse (*Economist*, September 28, 1929, p. 576).

The *Economist* (October 5, 1929, p. 616) published a report from its "Overseas Correspondent" dated September 25, 1929, that stated, "There have been several indications of 'protective' selling from your side in this market and of the transfer of funds to London as a result." The *Financial Times* of October 2, 1929 (p. 3), had a similar article: "Wall Street heard reports that London speculators were selling heavily here in order to raise funds to meet settlements in connection with the Hatry collapse."

Except for one minor article (October 9) dealing with Hatry's request for bail being refused, there were no articles about Hatry in the *New York Times* in October 1929. There were five articles in September, but nothing that was upsetting for the American investor in the New York Stock Exchange. The *Wall Street Journal* had minor articles in back pages on October 9 and October 16 that defined Hatry's difficulties and the liquidation of his firm. Both articles were less than three inches long and neither would be interpreted as important to an investor in the New York stock market. The selling as a result of the Hatry debacle took place in late September and early October, thus the October 24 crash was not directly linked to Hatry's misdeeds.

An interesting postscript is that it is said (Crisp, p. 57) an Anglo-American group wanted to buy United Steel and would have paid more than the cost to Austin Friar. Also, Austin would have been able to repay the loan in three more days (according to Hatry) or perhaps in six weeks. But without the loans repaid, the shares of Hatry's enterprises were depressed. To support the stock prices Hatry bought shares on the market, but this used up credit and substituted debt for equity during a period of depressed business activity. By September, the unsecured claims against Hatry's industrial complex had reached $67.5 million (unsecured does not necessarily mean bad claims).

There is little reason to think that the random selling by British investors to repay investment loans no longer covered by their Hatry investments would be enough to trigger the 1929 crash in the United States. While the Hatry affair was reported by the U.S. press, it did not receive the same level of publicity as "excessive speculation" received or the necessity to control the "speculators." The Hatry affair is an interesting anecdote.

THE HATRY COLLAPSE

The Hatry collapse was on the front page of the *New York Times* (September 21, 1929, p. 1): "London Stock Slump Brings Four Arrests." The *Economist* (September 28, 1929, p. 577) offered several numbers on which we can base some estimates of the loss magnitude. The external debts of Hatry's firms were approximately £12,550,000, and the share capital held by the outside public was £1.2 million (more information regarding this capital measure would have been helpful). The total public capital was £13,755,000.

The *New York Times* (December 17, 1929, p. 12) estimated the unsecured claims against Hatry's empire to be $67,500,000. Hatry used his personal wealth to support his stocks and by December 1929 his wealth was reduced to $6,250. He stated, "I took grave personal risks whereas I could so easily have let things go and walked off a free man." Stock firms in England were expected to lose as much as £1 million (*New York Times*, December 23, p. 32).

One of the loans obtained illegally was from Portchester Trust. Hatry stated, "The proceeds of the $1,045,175 loan from the Portchester Trust Ltd. were used in the general business of my group of companies. Neither I nor my co-directors have personally benefited from it. In fact, we have lost everything ourselves." These losses did not impress the sentencing judge.

Before the newspapers reported Hatry's financial difficulties, the stock prices of his firms collapsed (implying that insiders acted on their news). The major Hatry holdings fell to a small fraction of their high for the year (*Economist,* September 21, 1929, p. 531) before the news was released.

	Year's Highest Price*	September 19 Price*
Associated Automatic Machine Corporation	15/3	4/6
Corporation & General Securities	22/1½	5/0
Oak Investment Trust Shares	20/6	5/0
Photomaton Parent Corporation	15/7½	2/6
Retail Trade Securities Limited	16/0	2/6

*Prices in English pounds and shillings.

On September 21, dealings in Hatry's stocks were suspended.

Using an exchange rate of $4.70 we obtain an external unsecured capital exposure of $64,600,000 which is very close to the *New York Times* estimate of $67,500,000. The biggest portion of the exposure was debt ($59 million), and this debt was mostly owed to banks and other financial institutions, not to individuals.

The *New York Times* concluded (December 23, p. 32) that the banks and other financial institutions would bear the largest portion of the Hatry collapse and "the actual loss of the public will be relatively small." This reinforces the conclusion that the Hatry affair was not a major factor in the stock price collapses of October 24 and 29. There was not a significant number of individual investors who had to sell stock in New York in October because of Hatry in London in September.

A *New York Times* editorial lashed out at Hatry (December 19, p. 26): "Our Ponzis . . . simply are not in a class with the long succession of modern British adventurers and buccaneers of whom Clarence Hatry is the latest and, in terms of the havoc he has wrought, the greatest . . . the enormous Hatry vacuum compelled the withdrawal of London money from Wall Street and helped to precipitate our own October panic." There might have been some "other" call money that was withdrawn because of Hatry, but probably not a large amount of selling of stock.

CLARENCE C. HATRY

Hatry was born on December 16, 1888. His father was a silk merchant, and Hatry received a reasonable education (*Times*, London, June 12, 1965, p. 12). At age twenty-five he was a clerk in a London insurance office that sold insurance to emigrants from Italy, Poland, and Russia to the United States and Canada. By age thirty he was dealing in millions of pounds.

During his good years he and his family lived very well. His racehorse Furious, a 20-to-1 shot, won the Lincolnshire Handicap in 1920. He owned a $112,000 yacht (the Westward), and his wife had $1.4 million of jewelry. His house had a marble above-ground (upstairs) swimming pool, a glass-floored winter garden, and a cocktail bar built like a Tudor inn (*New York Times*, June 12, 1965, p. 31). The house had nine bathrooms.

His career was a series of successes followed by failures. He "inspired confidence by his amazing flair for getting investors a quick return for their money" (*New York Times*, December 17, 1929, p. 12). While larger than Ponzi, Hatry was in the same direction.

His first major corporate success was to gain control of the Commercial Bank of London. The bank failed in 1923–1924. Hatry personally covered the debts and guarantees of the bank. This action cost him $3.5 million (*New York Times*, September 21, 1929, p. 1). This was not exactly a Ponzi move.

He was jailed in September 1929 for the use of false collateral (fraud and forgery) and released in February 1938. On sentencing Hatry to fourteen years, Justice Avory stated, "His was the defense of any office boy who robbed a till to back a winner."

One of Hatry's codefendants, Albert E. Tabor, was released on £5,000 bail to spend Christmas with his wife and the baby son born while he was in jail (*New York Times*, December 22, 1929, p. 7). Hatry's three codefendants all had their jail terms shortened.

In 1939, after his release, Hatry published *Light Out of Darkness*, a book that he had written while imprisoned. He dedicated it:

> To all who are unemployed.
> To the oppressed of all nations, and
> To all who strive for peace.

His introduction included the statement (p. vii) "Nearly ten years ago my fellow countrymen by their decision gave me the opportunity to study the problem I now set before them." While he stated that he had "no resentment," it is clear that he achieved no resentment only with a great deal of effort.

In the book he offers a fifty-year world reconstruction plan. He saw the two primary problems of the world to be the maldistribution of population and the interdependence of nations (p. 10). "Nation is linked to nation in a network as intricate and as sensitive as a spider's web so that a tremor in any one part is felt everywhere."

He was concerned that many people lived in the wrong country, frequently because of won and lost wars (p. 18): "Frontiers made by war breed war. Those which embrace a true economic unity will provide the essential basis of prosperity, and the peace it brings."

Hatry's plan was simple to state:

1. transfer of people on a voluntary basis to where the economic opportunities are greater than where they are now
2. transfer of people on a voluntary basis to remove causes of political or racial dissension
3. transfer of lands so that countries could be self-sufficient
4. state supervision to regulate production

Obviously, each of the plan's elements gives rise to major problems and it is easy to be critical of the feasibility of their implementation, but in fairness to Hatry he was trying to solve difficult problems for which the solutions actually reached in 1939–1945 were much worse than those proposed by Hatry.

In jail he was the librarian, and he became an ardent booklover. Upon release from prison he opened a small book-trade business. This enterprise grew to the ownership of several publishing houses, twenty bookstores, a printing company, and two magazines. His firm went bankrupt in the 1950s. He then developed a chain of cleaning companies. He died on June 11, 1965, at the age of seventy-six.

CONCLUSIONS

The Hatry case was a tragedy. An aggressive businessman found himself in a situation where he hoped a desperate (and illegal) loan for three or four days would be sufficient to complete an economic transaction that would yield large benefits. While the entire affair was unfortunate for Hatry and for his creditors, it is very unlikely that we can blame Clarence Hatry for the 1929 New York stock market crash. The events were in that direction, but not significant enough in size to pass the test of primary causes. Also, the timing of events did not fit well. However, there is little question that the Hatry affair increased the level of anxiety significantly in England and marginally in the States, and it led some British investors to reduce their U.S. investments.

In January of 1930 Clarence Hatry and his three associates pleaded guilty to forgery and conspiracy. Hatry received a sentence of fourteen years of penal servitude. The other three penalties ranged from three to seven years. All four sentences included two years of hard labor.

On February 1, 1930, there was final settlement of the interests of the parties who had transactions suspended by the stock exchange when the scandal broke in September 1929. In 1937 there were attempts to obtain a pardon for Hatry. He was released in 1938. What sentence would you have given him?

CHAPTER 3

The Attempts to Stop the Speculators

During 1929 the public was bombarded with statements of outrage regarding the speculative orgy taking place on the New York Stock Exchange. If the media and respected people in authority say something often enough, a large percentage of the investing public is likely to believe it. By October 1929 the overall revealed opinion in the federal government was that there was excessive speculation in stocks and the market was too high. Galbraith (1961), Kindleberger (1978), and Malkiel (1996) all clearly accept the assumption that the market was too high. The *Federal Reserve Bulletin* of February 1929 stated that the Federal Reserve would restrain the use of "credit facilities in aid of the growth of speculative credit."

The U.S. Senate adopted a resolution stating that the Senate would support legislation "necessary to correct the evil complained of and prevent illegitimate and harmful speculation."

The president of the Investment Bankers Association of America (Trowbridge Callaway) gave a talk in which he spoke of "the orgy of speculation which clouded the country's vision."

John Kenneth Galbraith wrote (1961, pp. 16–19), "The mass escape into make-believe, so much a part of the true speculative orgy, started in earnest."

Adolph Casper Miller, an outspoken member of the Federal Reserve Board from its beginning and an influential member in 1929, described 1929 as "this period of optimism gone wild and cupidity gone drunk."

Senator Carter Glass asked, "What percentage of the public is [*sic*] speculating in the stocks of the stock exchange understand the real intrinsic value of the stocks in which they deal?" (Hearings of Senate Committee on Banking and Currency on Brokers' Loans, 1928).

A Senate committee (in reference to $3.8 billion of loans of the member banks of the New York Federal Reserve district on January 11, 1928) stated, "The largest part of this sum is used for speculation in the New York Stock Exchange" (Hearings of Senate Committee on Banking and Currency on Brokers' Loans, 1928).

Senator Robert LaFollette described "the great American evil of stock exchange gambling" (ibid., p. 2).

Senator Glass "proved" the speculative aspect: "It was selling at 108 in January. It was selling in the market yesterday at 69. Now what is that but gambling?" (ibid., p. 80).

National City Bank seemed to recommend a recession to solve the speculation problem: "A temporary slackening of the business pace, which would have as its effect a sobering influence on speculative sentiment, should be the very thing to keep business on a sound and enduring basis" (*National City Bank of New York Newsletter*, October 1929, p. 197).

An important letter from the Federal Reserve Board (February 2, 1929) to the member banks described "the extraordinary absorption of funds in speculative security loans."

Ferdinand Pecora asked, "What is the difference between speculation in stock and gambling in stock, to your notion?" Albert Henry Wiggin responded, "Investments that turn out wrong are speculations" (Committee on Banking and Currency, *Stock Exchange Practices*, 1933, pp. 2327 and 2418–19).

A Senate committee defined speculation: "Margin purchasing is speculation in securities with borrowed money" (Committee on Banking and Currency, *Stock Exchange Practices*, 1934, p. 9).

Myron C. Taylor, head of the U.S. Steel Corporation, described "the folly of the speculative frenzy that lifted securities to levels far beyond any warrant of supporting profits" (*Forbes*, December 15, 1929, p. 26).

The attacks on speculation were not limited to the United States.

In England, both the *Economist* (October 8, 1929, p. 774) and the *Financial Times* (October 4, 1929, p. 7) reported that Philip Snowden's remarks on speculation were widely quoted in the United States. They were reported by the *New York Times*, the *Wall Street Journal*, and the *Washington Post*. England's chancellor of the exchequer had referred to the "speculative orgy" in the United States.

Herbert Hoover's becoming President was a very significant event. He was a neighbor and good friend of Adolph Miller (see p. 29), and Miller reinforced Hoover's fears. President Hoover was an aggressive foe of speculation. For example, he later wrote, "I sent individually for the editors and publishers of major newspapers and magazines and requested them systematically to warn the country against speculation and the unduly high price of stocks." Hoover then pressured Secretary of the Treasury Mellon and the governor of the Federal Reserve Board (Roy Young) "to strangle the speculative movement." In his memoirs (1952) he titled his chapter 2 "We Attempt to Stop the Orgy of Speculation," his use of the specific words reflecting Snowden's influence.

The enemy was not clearly defined. The following groups are possibilities implied by the above quotations:

1. gamblers and speculators (neither term was well defined)

2. buyers of stock on margin

3. buyers of any stock in 1928 or 1929

4. buyers of risky stock

5. buyers of stock who sold at a gain after holding a short period of time

6. anyone who did business on Wall Street

Before placing blame on Hoover, consider the position of his rival for the 1932 presidency. Franklin Delanor Roosevelt in his 1930

campaign for the New York State governership unfairly attacked
Hoover's administration (*New York Times*, October 21, 1930):
"During the final period of inflation and stock market plunging not
one single step was taken by the responsible officials of the National
Administration to put on the brakes or to suggest even that the
situation was economically false and unsound." Thus Roosevelt
would have taken (or would have intended to take) even stronger
action to stop the "inflation" of stock prices.

By the time the crash arrived, a large percentage of the activity
on the market was in the odd lot purchases made by small investors
trying to buy into the American dream. Odd lot purchases had dou-
bled from 1924 to 1929 (*Times*, August 18, 1929, II, p. 7).

THE MONETARY POLICIES OF THE FEDERAL RESERVE BOARD

There is no question that the members of the Federal Reserve
Board were concerned with the level of the stock market and the
amount of speculation (see Bierman, 1991, pp. 71–99). They took
aggressive actions to suppress the speculation. By August 9, 1929,
the board had increased the discount rate to 6 percent. Friedman
and Schwartz (1963, p. 290) state, "There is no doubt that the desire
to curb the stock market boom was a major if not dominating factor
in Reserve actions in 1928 and 1929."

The futility of the board's efforts to stop the speculation by using
higher interest rates was described by Hamlin (a member of the
board in 1929): "When a speculative mania is once under way you
cannot do anything with it by the use of higher discount rates." A
6 percent borrowing rate is not going to discourage an investor who
expects an 18 percent stock price increase and a 3 percent dividend
yield.

The Fed made it difficult to finance securities with bank credit,
but prior to October 24, Black Thursday, the monetary situation
had eased significantly. For example, the *Economist*'s correspondent
was optimistic (October 16 report, October 26 issue, p. 766):
"There is no striking change in industrial or business news" and

"Call money has been distinctly easier, with the rate on the Stock Exchange as low as 5 per cent." Also: "Several of the largest member banks recently have been reported entirely out of debt to the Federal Reserve." And on page 776, "Brokers' loans are off $167 million." These are all upbeat observations reflecting an easing monetary situation one week before Black Thursday.

The *Magazine of Wall Street* (May 18, 1929) did not approve of the board's concern about speculation and astutely observed:

> However, if the attitude of the Federal Reserve officials can be properly construed from statements of its friends, there are those who are just as apprehensive that the market may go up as the average small investor is afraid it might go down.

In the search for the triggering event for the October 24 crash, the actions of the Federal Reserve do not loom large. If the objective is to find reasons why the crash resumed in 1930 and beyond, then the actions (or lack of actions) of the Federal Reserve become much more important. The actions of the Federal Reserve did not trigger the October 3 slide and the October 24 panic, though its actions and statements aimed at eliminating the rapid increase in stock prices.

The first page of the *New York Times* (October 15), in an article describing the Federal Reserve Board's survey of industrial and credit conditions, stated, "There was nothing in the board's survey to indicate that any pronounced change in credit policy was contemplated, and only passing reference was made to activities on the stock market." The *Wall Street Journal* (October 15, p. 1) had a headline "Reserve Policy Still Unformed" and went on to state "But Opinion is Growing that Stock Speculation Can Correct Itself." During the entire month of October the Federal Reserve Board had very low visibility.

The *Wall Street Journal* (November 2, 1929, p. 4) had an article describing the October actions of the Federal Reserve Board. It said that for some months the board had "pursued the policy of holding down loans of member banks in the securities markets." It achieved this by keeping member banks out of debt to their reserve banks. This policy led to the expansion of the loans by "others" during September and October.

Rappoport and White (1993) tie the cost of call money and brokers' loans to the existence of a price bubble in 1929. They point out:

1. the sharp divergence in growth of stock prices and dividends;

2. the premium on call and time brokers' loans were higher (2 to 3 percent) in 1928–1929 than in 1920–1927 (1 percent);

3. margin requirements on brokers' loans increased from 20 to 50 percent;

4. volatility of stock prices only rose after the crash, thus did not contribute to the premium.

From the above, Rappoport and White conclude that the existence of a price bubble was very likely. Liu, Santoni, and Stone (1995) disagree with Rappoport and White and conclude (p. 647), "The spread between brokers' loan rates and other money market rates cannot be used to confirm the possible existence of a stock market bubble during 1928–29." They offer three justifications for this conclusion. First, "A similar episode occurred in later 1919 and 1920, when stock prices were generally declining." Second, econometric tests provide no evidence of parameter instability or structural breaks in the spread." Third, "The relationship between the call and time brokers' loan rates during 1928/29 is inconsistent with the bubble explanation." Liu, Santoni, and Stone conclude (p. 654) that the spread that existed in 1928–1929 resulted from "the Fed's specific efforts to redirect bank lending away from loans collateralized by stocks and bonds." In a reply, White (1995) responded to these criticisms, but to some extent the criticisms are valid. That stock prices increased at a more rapid rate than dividends is an accepted fact (this is usually described as a decrease in dividend yield). But, a

Table 3.1
The Cost of Security Loans: 1929

Date	New York Stock Exchange Time Loans: 90 Days	Call Loans New	Renewal
October 5	9.13%	8.08%	8.20%
12	8.63	5.63	6.20%
19	7.75	6.28	6.40%
26	7.25	5.35	6.00%

decrease in dividend yield does not prove the existence of a bubble. The fact that stock price volatility did not increase until after the crash is a surprise, but does not prove there was a bubble. Actual volatility is merely eliminated as an explanation of the premium (expected volatility is still a contender).

The increase in margin requirements is consistent with excessive speculation and with stock prices being too high, but other explanations are also possible. The increase in the premium on the call loans is also consistent with the explanation offered by Liu, Santoni, and Stone (1995) that the Fed was exerting pressure. It is also consistent with increased perceived risk or increased real risk. Thus, there are several plausible explanations, but the evidence is not conclusive that when money on the street costs more than credit in general, stocks are too high.

THE COST OF A MARGIN ACCOUNT

During 1929 common stock dividend yields were slightly above 3 percent on the average. Table 3.1 shows the loan costs that the margin account stock buying investor was facing in October 1929 (Wigmore, 1985, p. 627).

While the loan costs were high compared to the average common stock dividend yield, they were not high compared to the 1921 to 1929 stock price increases. Also, these rates reflected the August increase in the discount rate imposed by the Federal Reserve Board.

After October 5, the call loan rates are all low compared to the investment opportunities available during the same time period in London, England.

THE 1928 SENATE HEARINGS

The Senate Committee on Banking and Currency held hearings in February and March 1928 on broker loans. The House Committee on Banking and Currency held hearings on stabilization in March, April, and May 1928. Both sets of hearings are important in establishing the attitudes of Congress towards the stock market. Also, the hearings were likely to have influenced the Federal Reserve Board and its pronouncements.

The Senate committee was concerned that the level of loans secured by stocks and bonds exceeded $3.8 billion and that these loans were "used for speculation in the New York Stock Exchange" (Senate Committee, 1928, p. 1). Senator Glass asked Edmund Platt, the vice governor of the Federal Reserve Board, "Do you think the bets are always made with reference to the soundness of the security?" (Senate Committee, 1928, pp. 79–80).

The most interesting component of the House committee's hearings (1928) was the exchange between Adolph Miller, a very influential forceful member of the Federal Reserve Board, and Otis Wingo, congressman from Arkansas. Wingo wanted Miller to understand that "The factor that should control in fixing the rediscount rates and in determining whether or not you will put more money in the market or take money out is not what is going on in the stock market that is not the prime consideration, but what are the necessities of legitimate business" (Hearings of House Committee on Banking and Currency on Stabilization, 1928, p. 118). Wingo then added, "And the fact that in meeting the necessities of legitimate business you happen to stimulate a little bit the amount of speculation in the stock market should not deter you from meeting the major needs of business." Miller did not understand the point being made. Miller was obsessed with need to control "speculative loans."

Pedersen (1961, p. 494) studied the period 1919–1932 and concluded, "The U.S. authorities precipitated the crisis by the crusade against speculation instead of leaving stock prices to their fate and supporting the expansion of economic activity." There is a large element of validity in this conclusion, but perhaps there are other factors that should be included as causes of the 1929 market crash.

ANDREW W. MELLON

Mellon was secretary of the treasury in 1929. Given the pressure being exerted by President Hoover we have to admire the restraint and wisdom of Mellon's public statements. On January 1, 1929, he issued a New Year's message that industry and business were on a sound basis and made an optimistic prediction for 1929 (*New York Times*, January 1, p. 26). The statement was buried in the back pages. Later in the year but before the crash he stated (*Times*, March 15, p. 1) that it was a good time to buy bonds (they were at a low price in March).

On October 29, 1928, the *Wall Street Journal* (p. 18) had a major article, "Why Mellon Did Not Resign." The article described his fight with President Hoover over Federal Reserve policy regarding the stock market. While the Fed is not controlled by the President, Hoover had a friend, Adolph Miller, who was on the board, with whom he regularly conversed. Miller and Hoover reinforced each other's convictions that the speculators had to be stopped. Mellon was more concerned with the real economy and was not happy with Miller's influence with the President and with the board. Despite this basic disagreement regarding the attempts by the Fed to bring about a decrease in stock prices, Hoover convinced Mellon to remain as secretary of the treasury.

Senator J. T. Robinson (a Democrat) attributed the stock market crash to Mellon's optimistic statements on market conditions (*New York Times*, October 31, 1929, p. 3). Senator A. K. Robinson (a Republican) defended Mellon's statements (*Times*, November 2, 1929, p. 2).

With Hoover conducting a campaign against speculators, Mellon's statements are very reasonable. One cannot find statements from the Treasury in 1929 that would have either upset an investor or encouraged a speculator. In a difficult time period Mellon did well.

AFTER 1929

President Franklin Roosevelt continued the fight against the "dishonest" financiers and the "speculators." Thus in 1937 the *New York Times* headlined (November 6, 1937, p. 1) "Roosevelt Calls Speculators Dangerous." The article made several interesting points. First was a Roosevelt quote aimed at both speculators and news reporters: "Speculation in news stories is just as dangerous as speculation in the stock market." It seems the administration had received letters "criticizing the administration for permitting certain stocks to drop in value." With the "new deal" some thought stocks would only go up.

This position was easy to understand given the promises of the administration. As one high official stated, attempting to explain the impossible, the President's purpose, "if any, was to make it clear that speculators deserved to suffer, while [those] who invested conservatively were to be protected." The insertion of "if any" was great. It is unfortunate that the name of the high official was not revealed.

The article continued, "The Administration's policy to make capital investment more attractive and speculation as unattractive as possible was illustrated by the trend of all New Deal regulatory measures pertaining to the stock market, this official said." Imagine the government official attempting to distinguish between an investment and a speculation in the capital market for the purpose of assessing a fine or defining a crime.

CONCLUSIONS

Bierman (1991) has a more complete description of the thoughts and motivations of the members of the Federal Reserve Board. It is clear that the board in 1929 thought that the use of bank credit for speculation was bad and that the stock market was too high. But the board did not do anything in September or October 1929 that can be pointed to as a trigger of the 1929 crash. They would have liked to have had stock prices decline a bit, but except for Adolph Miller (described by Hamlin as wanting a "sudden liquidation and crash"), they did not seek a crash. Hamlin stated regarding the February 2 letter of the board: "The board did not desire by that warning to bring about any radical deflation of speculative loans. It wanted gradually to attempt to put federal reserve credit back where it belonged, and take it out as a basis of these excessive speculative loans" (U.S. Senate Committee on Banking and Currency Hearings, January 1931, and Hamlin's diary of February 5, 1929).

My position is that the efforts to stop the speculation created a climate that merely required a slight push or a spark to set off the selling panic. Thus, the smoking gun starting the crash might be events relatively minor in themselves but major in their consequences.

CHAPTER 4

The Week of March 25, 1929

Secretary of the Treasury Mellon opened 1929 with a statement for the January 1 newspapers. The *New York Times* (p. 26) headed a column with "Mellon Optimistic on Business Trend." His comments were eagerly awaited by the investment community. Mellon did not make frequent announcements. The *Times* said the comments were awaited "with unusual interest because of the unprecedented speculative activities on the Stock Exchange." The closest Mellon came to commenting on the state of the stock market was in reference to interest rates: "High interest rates in the open market, due to the speculation on the Stock Exchange, forced the Treasury during the year to pay 4¾ per cent in selling one of its short-term issues."

In February the Federal Reserve Board sent out its famous letter dated February 2, 1929, to all Federal Reserve banks. The objective was to tell all members banks that a bank could not use the rediscount facilities at its Federal Reserve Bank "when it borrows either for the purpose of making speculative loans or for the purpose of maintaining speculative loans." This letter alerted the participants of the New York Stock Exchange that the board believed that there was too much stock market speculation. Member banks were urged not to borrow from the Federal Reserve Bank to finance stock market speculation.

On the afternoon of February 14 the Federal Reserve Bank of New York voted, on its own initiative, to increase the rediscount rate from 5 to 6 percent. By 6:40 p.m., the Federal Reserve Board passed a resolution that "moved that the Board disapprove of the action of the directors of the Federal Reserve Bank of New York and determine the rate of that bank to be five percent."

The board did not want borrowers (borrowing to finance speculative loans) who could pay the increased rate to have access to bank funds. It wanted the loans to be rejected because they were speculative and not accepted because the borrowers could pay the higher interest rate. The New York Fed wanted the cost of the funds to regulate who borrowed the funds and did not want to distinguish between investment and speculative purposes.

On March 12 the *New York Times* (p. 44) had an important article regarding an announcement from the Treasury Department: "Mellon Not to Act in Speculation Ban." The "ban" referred to the February letter from the board. The rumor on Wall Street was that Mellon opposed the distribution of the letter. Now, the announcement indicated that the Treasury would not "revise Fed's war on speculation." There was no reference to the availability of credit. This announcement was good news for Wall Street since Mellon did not reinforce the Fed's war against speculators. On the other hand, neither did Mellon repudiate it.

The Mellon announcement triggered a classic letter from a concerned lawyer (I. M. Levy). In a letter dated March 12 (in the *Times*, March 28, p. 20) Levy wrote, "Prosperity is very much a matter of psychology and if the Federal Reserve Board continues its pessimistic note, it may create a panic."

Mellon's response a couple of days later was not up to his normal standards. He made the point to Levy that Levy probably meant newspapers and others were pessimistic, but not the Federal Reserve Board. To top it off he sent a copy of the Federal Reserve Board's letter to Levy to "prove" his point.

I fear that Mr. Levy was not reassured by the secretary's letter. It is interesting how perceptive Levy's was. This letter was before both the March and October crashes. In fairness, Mellon responded as well as he could, given his sensitive position. It was reasonable for him to deny that any federal government employee or body was pessimistic. Of course, the culprit being attacked by the board was speculation. The board was not obviously pessimistic from Mellon's viewpoint, which focused on economic activity.

On March 15 the *New York Times* (p. 1) had a headline "Mellon Advises Buying of Bonds By Investors." Mellon cited the relatively high bond yields and low prices compared to high stock prices. "This does not mean that many stocks are not good investments. Some, however, are too high in price to be good buys." He then said, "For prudent investors . . . now is the time to buy good bonds." The article then went on to explain why Mellon's mild statement with regard to the investment climate was important. The Federal Reserve Board had declared "warfare against the excessive use of Federal Reserve credit for speculative activities on the Stock Exchange," and Mellon had only said that some stocks were too high in price. The news article revealed that Mellon "would not enter into a general discussion of present-day speculation in stocks" and that he had a long conference with Hoover on the day before his statement.

Some cynics suggested that Mellon's recommendation to buy bonds was related to the Treasury's efforts to sell low-yielding treasuries, but this is unfair and we can assume that it was Mellon's way of saying some, but not all, stocks were too high.

Given that we know Hoover's position with regard to speculation during 1929 (he wanted it checked), we can conject what types of statements Hoover requested from Mellon. At a minimum he wanted a statement describing the evils of stock market speculation. Instead he got a reasoned statement, that with hindsight we can conclude was good investment advice.

The next day the editorial in the *New York Times* (March 16, p. 18) led off with "The most significant thing in Secretary Mellon's comment on stock market prices is the fact that he made any comment at all." The *Times* would also have liked a blast at speculation, but not having received it, the editor evaluated Mellon's comments to be "a weighty statement" that described the "dangers of excessive speculation." If Mellon had wanted to say this, his statement would have included these words or something close to them. Rather Mellon gave an intelligent evaluation and sensible recommendations.

On March 16 Roy Young, governor of the Federal Reserve Bank and chairman of the Federal Reserve Board, spoke before the Commercial Club of Cincinnati. His speech made clear that the Federal Reserve Board advocated the rationing of credit for securities: "It seems to me that it would be the part of prudence for all who are lenders to see first that business gets credit at reasonable rates and let the others get what is left." The "others" are the financial community, including the buyers of the stocks and bonds issued by the business that Young wants to help.

On Tuesday, March 26, there was a *New York Times* first page major headline, "Stock Prices Break Heavily as Money Soars to 14 Per Cent." The *Times* conjectured that the market crash on Monday was caused by an expectation of drastic action by the Federal Reserve Board, including the possibility of an increase in the rediscount rate. The 14 percent cost of call money was very high (in October 1929 the cost of call money was 5 percent).

There was an interesting footnote to the day's trading. Radio (RCA) went up 4¼ points as the market went down. International Telephone and Telegraph also went "against the tide" increasing by 6⅞ points.

The analyst of the *Times* offered three reasons for the crash.

1. The tight money. The increase in the cost of call money from 9 percent to 14 percent shocked the market. The 14 percent was the highest rate since July 1, 1920.

2. The fear that the Fed would increase the rediscount rate or do something else to dry up credit to finance securities.

3. There were too many speculative positions.

The article said the speculators were "prone to do the wrong thing at the right time, or the right thing at the wrong time." One suspects that the reporter was actually thinking of investors new to the stock market rather than the conventional expert manipulators that Washington looked at as speculators.

The article on the price break referred to "Hundreds of Margins" being called. In the past the margin calls had been sent by the mail, but in March 1929, in the new high tech world, they were sent by telegraph. This reference to margin calls highlights the fact that the lenders intended to either get additional cash backing for the margin loans or sell the securities. One has to assume that many securities were sold as a result of the margin calls since not all the investors had additional cash.

The next day's market performance (Tuesday, March 26) was even worse than that of Monday. The Wednesday *Times* (p. 1) in its right-hand headline exclaimed, "Stocks Crash and Then Rally in 8,246,740 Share Day: Money Goes to 20 Per Cent."

The volume of trading beat the previous day's record by 1,292,700 shares. The average market price dropped 9.6 percent.

At an interest cost of 20 percent few or no rational investors could maintain a margin account. In fact, some broker loans were at 22 percent. In addition, there was a shortage of available loan funds even at these interest rates. Funds to finance securities were not available.

For the second day bond prices were lower on March 26. This was partially the result of convertible bonds selling at lower prices reflecting lower stock prices, but it was also the result of investors being in a state of shock regarding securities in general. During the day, three hundred stock issues hit new lows for the year. Interestingly, in this down market Radio was up 1⅛ points closing at $93 (the high for the year to this date was 109⅜ and the low was 68¼). Obviously, Radio was a stock immune to market fluctuations because of its underlying strength (in October this obvious conclusion will turn out to be wrong).

One of the subheadlines on page one (*New York Times*, Wednesday, March 27) was "Bankers Aid Recovery." The assistance of the bankers had occurred towards the end of the day (Tuesday, March 26).

On Wednesday, March 27, the market recovered some of its

losses. In a left-hand page one headline of Thursday, March 28 ("recoveries" are not as important as "crashes," thus the recovery had a downgraded headline), the *New York Times* had "Stocks Rally Vigorously As Bankers Aid Market; All Needed Funds Ready," "Call Money 15 Per Cent," and "National City Bank Offers $25,000,000 in 5 Lots."

The National City Bank offer to lend $25 million is very interesting. The bank was part white knight and part profit-maximizing bank. It offered to lend $5 million at 16 percent. If more funds were needed it would lend $5 million more at 17 percent. For the fifth $5 million unit it would charge 20 percent. The bank was acting as a lender of last resort, but at these high rates it was not exactly encouraging investment in stocks.

The chairman of National City Bank was Charles Mitchell.

As a result of Mitchell's decisive actions, or because of good fortune, the market did not continue its drop on March 27. In fact, the events of March 25 and 26 pale in comparison to the events of October. But still the sequence of events in March is very important.

Mitchell was castigated by congressmen of both houses for his actions that were said to indicate contempt of the Federal Reserve Board. Mitchell was not the only banker who took steps to stem the stock price fall. The New York Federal Reserve Bank (Governor George Harrison) also supplied liquidity to member banks so that they could finance brokers. Harrison wanted the New York Federal Reserve Bank to be "in the position of freely lending money at its going rate in order that there might not be any charge that it had arbitrarily refused or rationed credit." But rationing credit is exactly what the Federal Reserve Board wanted the Federal Reserve banks to do. Harrison's position was that the Federal Reserve Bank should "grant credit on eligible paper." Obviously, he did not want to analyze whether the purpose of the borrowing was for investment or speculation.

Rightly or wrongly, Mitchell was given credit by the Federal Reserve Board (especially board member Adolph Miller), the press, and Congress for reversing the stock market crash of March. On page one, the headline of the *Times* (March 29) was "Glass Assails Mitchell For Bank's Aid to Market; Stocks Up in Buying Rush."

"Glass" was Senator Carter Glass of Virginia. Glass called for Mitchell's resignation as a director of the New York Federal Reserve Bank. He denounced Mitchell's "contempt of [the] Board." Glass's position was heartily supported by other senators.

When informed of Glass's denouncement of him and his bank's actions, Mitchell said, "That's very interesting, but I have no comment to make."

On the same day (Friday, March 29) the *Times* reported that Radio was up to 106½ and that the cost of call money had dropped from 15 to 8 percent. Obviously, the National City Bank's offer to lend at 16 to 20 percent did not cause this drop.

On March 28 Adolph Miller, a senior member of the Federal Reserve Board, was in New York to have lunch and attend a meeting with the board of directors of the New York Federal Reserve Bank. Mitchell was a board member. Miller did not at all want to have lunch with Mitchell, nor did he want to meet with him. After much persuasion from George Harrison, and after Miller called Governor Young, Miller went to the meeting (we assume he also went to lunch).

On Friday, March 29, Congress announced that an inquiry would take place. The *New York Times* right-hand headline (March 30, p. 1) said, "Congress Inquiry Likely Into Stock Speculation; Mitchell Explains Stand." It was not clear whether Congress was more upset about stocks going up, the existence of speculators, or the thought that Mitchell's bank stopped the price decline. Senator Brookhart of Iowa made page two of the *Times* with the statement that he "would forbid the widespread use of banking resources in speculation."

Mitchell's explanation of why he thought the Federal Reserve Board's February letter did not apply to his bank in March was that the National City Bank, at the time, was not in debt to the Fed, thus not restricted in its actions.

The April issue of the *Federal Reserve Bulletin* describes the ongoing policy of restraining the diversion of bank credit into speculative uses but does not mention the stock market drop of March 25 and March 26.

THE BANKING ACT OF 1933

The Banking Act of 1933 is a law of the United States. It includes the words "to prevent a repetition of the incident in March 1929, when despite the express warning of the Federal Reserve Board to the contrary, the National City Bank poured $25,000,000 into the call-loan market." The act gives the Federal Reserve Board the power to prevent member banks from disregarding the wishes of the board (*Stock Exchange Practices*, 1934, p. 18).

Of course, National City Bank did not "pour" $25 million into the call-loan market. It offered to make loans at very high rates. Since National City Bank had not borrowed from the Fed, the Banking Act of 1933, if in place, would not have stopped National City Bank from acting just as it acted. Also, it is not clear that we would want to prevent National City Bank from taking the actions it took.

THE 1931 SENATE HEARINGS

In hearings conducted by the U.S. Senate Committee on Banking and Currency in 1931 to review the performance of the Federal Reserve system, Governor Harrison of Federal Reserve Bank of New York said he had never asked member banks in New York to reduce their loans to brokers. The Federal Reserve Bank used interest rates to ration capital rather than to give "a particular admonition to particular banks." While not exactly accurate, since elements of "direct action" can be found in the actions of the New York Fed in 1929, it does describe how Harrison wished to operate his bank. Harrison, in turn, would not try to tell Mitchell's National City Bank whom to lend to and at what rate.

THE 1933 STOCK EXCHANGE PRACTICES
HEARINGS (1933)

Mitchell was questioned extensively by Ferdinand Pecora, counsel for the committee, at the 1933 stock exchange practices hearings conducted by the subcommittee of the U.S. Senate Committee on Banking and Currency.

Pecora wanted to establish that Mitchell's action in March 1929 was "a flaunt on the warning sounded by the Federal Reserve Board." Mitchell pointed out that at the time "We were not borrowing a penny from the Federal Reserve Bank, and not rediscounting . . ." and that rates had gone up to "15 or 16 percent. We stopped them to allay what was becoming a money panic, an inability of the legitimate borrower to borrow for his day contracts the money that was essential."

Senator Brookhart then asked, "Who were those honest borrowers? Weren't they speculators?" Mitchell explained they were brokers. Brookhart interrupted to say, "That was a speculative contract. It was one of those gambling deals, wasn't it?"

Mitchell then explained the purpose of a bank's lending to a broker and that National City Bank wished "to avoid a general collapse of the securities market."

Pecora then placed the blame on Mitchell: "If you had let it collapse in March that would have saved hundreds of thousands of dollars to people who invested later on."

Mitchell said he wanted "to stop a money panic." Brookhart modified his thought to "Nobody is going to stop this speculation."

The misconceptions of the senators were immense. The chairman (Senator Norbeck) asked of Mitchell, "How much higher did they go before they broke off—by three or four times, some of them, didn't they?" This unrealistic view of the market was not uncommon, but it is shocking.

Mitchell was asked by the chairman, "It has been repeatedly interpreted by Senator Glass as your saying to the Federal Reserve Board to go to hell. Isn't that so?" Mitchell agreed that Senator Glass "took that attitude," but it was not the result "of any statement made by me, but as the result of the newspaper article." Mitchell pointed out that the Federal Reserve Bank of New York was kept informed of the actions of National City Bank and did not object to its actions.

CONCLUSIONS

The March 25–26, 1929, stock market price declines were a dry run for October. The March declines were probably triggered by the high cost of call money. Mitchell and National City Bank received credit for stopping the selling panic and saving the day, but we cannot be sure of the effect of National City's offer to lend $25 million. The bank loans were to be at 16 percent to 20 percent interest cost. At these rates investors could not hold stocks with confidence. The turnabout in stock market prices might have resulted from Mitchell's offer to lend, or it could be that the good business news could not be ignored and at the lower prices investors stepped in and bought.

There is one thing that the New York bankers learned. Washington would be very upset if the banks repeated the actions of National City Bank in any future crash. Surprisingly, in October the New York banks did try to stop the crash.

After March the stock market resumed its climb, reaching its peak in September. This was looked at by Washington as the result of more speculation. Washington thought the additional speculation was made feasible by Mitchell (actually Harrison and the New York Federal Reserve Bank deserved a large share of the credit). By September the market had risen above the March level, thus had further to fall and the consequences would be more severe. Mitchell was blamed for the more severe consequences.

In October when the real crash happened, the actions taken by the banks were not effective in stopping it. It is not obvious that National City Bank acted decisively or effectively in March, but many people (especially those in Washington) thought it did. They also thought the action was ill-considered. In October they would learn that not even the powerful Wall Street bankers could stem the tide of a selling panic.

CHAPTER 5

Significant News and Dates in the Month of October 1929

This chapter will review on a sample basis the news that an investor had access to in the month of October and attempt to relate the news to the significant events for that month.

The headlines or headings for the news items that accompany each date were selected because they were the biggest print, the most interesting news, or the most relevant news. The first set of news is always from the front page of the *New York Times* and the second set from the *Times*'s financial section. For each of the significant market dates news items were extracted for several days preceding the relevant market date and one day after. The objective is to give a feeling for the type of information a reasonably well-informed investor had available. The reader will find useful information for investment decisions to be scarce. Remember, when the relevant market date is X, the relevant paper date will be (X+1).

The first relevant market date is October 3. This date marked the year's worst break in stock prices (to that date).

RELEVANT MARKET DATE: THURSDAY, OCTOBER 3

Paper of Tuesday, October 1 (p. 1)

"$75,000,000 of Tax Favors to Friends of Tammany" (Note: New York City Mayor Jimmy Walker took care of his friends.)

"Rocket Plane Soars in Uncanny Flight" (Note: The German plane only went a few hundred yards and crashed on landing.)

"Hoover Leadership on Tariff Depends on One or Two Votes" (Note: The tariff is the Smoot-Hawley Tariff, and the issue is whether or not the President will have duty-fixing powers.)

Finance Section (p. 36)

"Renewed Decline in Stocks—With Partial Recovery"

"Call Money 10%"

"The Cost of Speculation" (Note: The article dealt with the cost of carrying securities compared to the smaller average dividend yield of stocks.)

Paper of Wednesday, October 2 (p. 1)

"Hoover Selects M'Nab to Rebuild Dry Law Machinery" (Note: Prohibition was still in place.)

"71-Story Skyscraper to Rise in Wall St. Area" (Note: Real estate was still booming in Manhattan.)

Finance Section (p. 40)

"Another Break in Stocks, With Irregular Recovery"

"Hung Up With Stock" (Note: The article described investment pools holding stocks that had gone down.)

Paper of Thursday, October 3 (p. 1)

"Dr. Stresemann Dies Suddenly in Berlin" (Note: The doctor was a highly respected statesman, and his death opened the way for the Nazi rise.)

Finance Section (p. 40)

"Recovery in Stocks, Some Later Reaction"

"Restrained Optimism"

Paper of Friday, October 4 (p. 1)

"MacDonald to be Greeted by City Today" (Note: The Labor Party leader, Ramsay MacDonald, the prime minister of England, was well liked by the U.S. press.)

"Year's Worst Break Hits Stock Market" (Note: This was the third or fourth lead story on p. 1.)

Finance Section (p. 36)

"Heavy Break in Stocks"

"Call Money at 6%"

"Fear at the Helm" (Note: This article discussed the high level of broker loan accounts and reported the "orgy of American speculation" talk by Philip Snowden, the British chancellor of the exchequer.)

"Utilities Hard Hit" (Note: The article noted that the hit coincided with the reopening of hearings regarding utilities conducted by the Federal Trade Commission in Washington.)

"Brokers' Loans Up $43,000,000 in Week" (Note: The level of brokers' loans was looked at as one of the most significant types of stock market information.)

The *Washington Post* of October 4 with a page one headline exclaimed, "Stock Prices Crash in Frantic Selling." The *New York Times* (p. 1) cited three contributing factors:

1. a large broker loan increase was expected (the article stated that the loans increased, but the increase was not as large as expected);

2. the statement by Philip Snowden, England's chancellor of the exchequer, that described America's stock market as a "speculative orgy";

3. weakening of margin accounts making it necessary to sell, which further depressed prices.

While the 1929 financial press focused extensively on broker loans and margin account activity, the Snowden statement is the only significant unique financial news event on October 3. The October 4 issue of the *Wall Street Journal* (p. 20) also reported the remark by Snowden that there was "a perfect orgy of speculation." Also on October 4, the *New York Times* had a major editorial on Snowden's speculation orgy comment. On Sunday, October 6, the *Times* (p. 4E) made another editorial reference to Snowden's American speculation orgy comment. It added that "Wall Street had come to recognize its truth." The editorial also quoted Secretary of the Treasury Mellon that investors "acted as if the price of securities would infinitely advance." The *Times* editor obviously thought there was excessive speculation and agreed with Snowden.

On October 24, 1930, the *New York Times* (p. 22) had a letter that identified Snowden as a socialist who spoke and acted as a capitalist. On October 26, 1930 (p. 3 of the *New York Times Magazine*), a very favorable extensive article on Snowden said that his political enemies described him as a "monster of communism." It is interesting that an Englishman of the political left fired the first successful shot against the speculators that the American right was targeting.

The stock market fell on October 3 and October 4, but almost all reported business news was very optimistic. The primary negative news items were the statements by Snowden and Mellon regarding the amount of speculation in the American stock market. The market had been subjected to a barrage of statements throughout the year that there was excessive speculation and that the level of stock prices was too high. The *Washington Post* (October 16, p. 14) described the market as "nervous." There is a strong possibility that the Snowden comment reported on October 4 was the push that started the boulder down the hill.

The next most relevant market date is October 16. The stock declines on this date and dates to follow reflect the adverse news regarding public utility regulation.

RELEVANT MARKET DATE: THE NEXT SIGNIFICANT MARKET DATE IS WEDNESDAY, OCTOBER 16.

Paper of Saturday, October 5 (p. 1)

"Senators Defeat Hoover Plan Again on Tariff Board" (Note: This dealt with the composition of the tariff commission of the Smoot-Hawley Tariff Act.)

Finance Section (p. 26)

"Stocks Decline Sharply"

"Call Money in Abundance"

Paper of Sunday, October 6 (p. 1)

"World Peace Talks Begun"

"Brisk Rally Checks Long Market Drop"

Finance Section (p. 119)

"Ready to Resume Utility Hearings" (Note: This was the Federal Trade Commission conducting hearings regarding utility mergers.)

"Indices of Business Mostly Favorable"

"Loans to Brokers Big Market Factor" (Note: The article explained that the figures are designed to show how much credit was used for speculation.)

Paper of Monday, October 7

Finance Section (pp. 35–39)

"Business in West Holding Up Well"

Paper of Tuesday, October 8 (p. 1)

"McDonald Tells Senate Wars Are Over if Kellogg Pact Is Made Effective" (Note: He was wrong.)

"Mellon Will Stay in Office Till 1933: Wall Street Heartened" (Note: Andrew Mellon was the secretary of treasury and well liked by Wall Street.)

Finance Section (p. 38)

"Recovery in Stocks Continue"

"Guessing the Next Move" (Note: Cites the chartists that stocks should recover 25 percent of the September loss.)

"The Reasons for Cheaper Money"

Paper of Wednesday, October 9

"Athletics Win 3–1" (Note: Howard Emke of Philadelphia beat the Chicago Cubs in first game of World Series.)

Paper of Thursday, October 10 (p. 1)

"Hoover and MacDonald Join in Saying War Between U.S. Is Now 'Unthinkable' "

"Athletics Win 9–3" (Note: Foxx and Simmons hit home runs.)

"Independence Move for the Philippines Lost in Tariff Row" (Note: Those congressmen in favor of Philippine independence were having trouble bringing the issue to a vote.)

Finance Section (p. 40)

"General Decline in Stocks"

"Call Money Goes to 5%" (Note: The cost of call money was very low.)

Paper of Friday, October 11

Finance Section (pp. 45–50)

"Stocks Advance"

"Foreign Sell Still Heavy"

"Brokers' Loans Cut $91,000,000 in Week"

"U.S. Steel Shows Rise in Bookings"

"Our Exports Show Big Gain in August: Increase for 8 Months"

Paper of Saturday, October 12 (p. 1)

"Cubs Triumph 3–1" (Note: Bush wins. Dykes has three hits.)

"Government Would Accept Morgan Yacht, But $100,000 Yearly Upkeep is Problem" (Note: The yacht was a gift from J. P. Morgan.)

Finance Section (p. 27)

"Many Stocks Advance . . . Easy Money Develops"

"Bars Stock Split by Boston Edison" (Note: This is the famous Massachusetts' Commission decision.)

Paper of Sunday, October 13 (p. 1)

"Athletics Score 10 in 7th, Beat Cubs 10–8"

Finance Section (p. 14N)

"Steel Figures a Surprise: Instead of a Sizable Decline an Increase of 244,370 tons was published" (Note: Another cause for optimism.)

Paper of Monday, October 14 (p. 1)

"Tariffs Will Be Rewritten" (Note: Smoot-Hawley moves closer to passing. This is a barrier to world trade.)

Paper of Tuesday, October 15 (p. 1)

"Athletics Win Title: 3-Run Rally in Ninth Beats the Cubs, 3–2"

"Hoover is Cheered at Baseball Game"

"Reserve Board Finds No Ebb in Business"

Finance Section (pp. 41–43)

"Regular Decline in Most Stocks"

"Call Money 6%"

"The Boston Decision" (Note: The Massachusetts' Commission had rejected Boston Edison's request and this was reported on October 12.)

"AT&T Sets Record for 9 Months' Net"

Paper of Wednesday, October 16 (p. 1)

"Byrd Opens Spring Drive of Discovery" (Note: Commander Byrd is exploring Antarctica.)

Finance Section (pp. 40–42)

"Confused Movements Dominate Trading . . ."

"Mitchell Asserts Stocks are Sound" (Note: Charles Mitchell is chairman of National City Bank of New York.)

"Inquiry Ordered In Boston Edison" (Note: This is a very important news article.)

Paper of Thursday, October 17 (p. 1)

"130 Dry Raiders Sweep Along Coast"

Finance Section (pp. 38–60)

"Stocks Decline Sharply in Active Trading"

"Charges Utilities Withheld Data" (FTC)

The next relevant market date is Black Thursday, October 24. There is no "news trigger," but there is a major price slide on October 23, anticipating the October 24 crash.

RELEVANT MARKET DATE: THURSDAY, OCTOBER 24 (BLACK THURSDAY)

Paper of Friday, October 18 (p. 1)

"Rum Ring Paid Big Bribes"

Finance Section (pp. 37–41)

"Stocks Break Again, Then Recover Sharply"

"Brokers' Loans Drop by $80,000,000 in Week"

Paper of Saturday, October 19 (p. 1)

"Record $564,773,252 budget" (Note: The budget is for New York State and Governor Roosevelt.)

"Foreigners Flee to River Gunboats in Chinese Mutiny"

Finance Section (pp. 26–27)

"Early Recovery in Stocks, Then Heavy Breaks"

"Call Money 5%"

"Little to Support Prices"

"The Return to Reason" (Note: Celebrating the stock price drops.)

"Huge Drop in Month in Exchange Stocks" (Note: Stocks lost $2.6 billion in September. The market value at the beginning of October was $87 billion.)

Paper of Sunday, October 20 (p. 1)

"Stocks Driven Down as Wave of Selling Engulfs the Market"

"J. L. Livermore Reported to be Head of Group Hammering High-Priced Securities" (Note: Livermore was famous for selling short.)

Finance Section (p. N7)

"Easy Credit in View for Rest of Year"

Paper of Monday, October 21 (p. 1)

"Drift of Voters to Thomas Does Not Disturb Tammany" (Note: Norman Thomas was the most famous U.S. Socialist. Tammany is a subset of New York City Democrats. The "bosses.")

Finance Section (pp. 37–46)

"German Business Reported Lagging"

"Europe Recalling Capital From Here: London Has Sold Stocks"

"French Investors Selling High-Priced Stocks"

"German Market Helped by Return of European Capital From America"

"Steel Production Ebbs in the Week: Car Building is Heavy"

Paper of Tuesday, October 22 (p. 1)

"Stocks Slump Again, But Rally at Close"

Finance Section (p. 39)

"Stocks Break Again; Third Largest Trading on Record"

"Call Money 5%"

"Heavy Margin Calls" (Note: On p. 44, General Electric reported increased earnings as well as 29 percent increase in orders received.)

Paper of Wednesday, October 23 (p. 1)

"Stocks Gain Sharply But Slip Near Close: Market Gloom Lessened"

Finance Section (p. 38)

"Stocks Recover Sharply at Opening"

"Sentiment More Cheerful" (Note: There was an article indicating that Roger W. Babson had said to sell [October 22]. "Babson's frequent statements to sell do not usually command much attention in Wall Street.")

On Wednesday, October 23, the prices of stocks crashed. But this date is not usually noted since the sell-off on Thursday, October 24, was even more severe.

Paper of Thursday, October 24 (p. 1)

"Prices of Stocks Crash: Paper Loss $4,000,000,000" (Note: This crash was the day before Black Thursday.)

"College Sport Tainted by Bounties" (Note: Student athletes were recruited and given perks.)

Finance Section (p. 38–44)

"Margin Calls" (Note: "What Wall Street described as an avalanche of margin calls went out of the financial district last night.")

"Demand for Steel Generally Large"

Paper of Friday, October 25 (p. 1)

"Worst Stock Crash Stemmed by Banks" (Note: This headline was on the right-hand side of first page.)

"Treasury Officials Blame Speculation"

Finance Section (pp. 41–46)

"Panicky Liquidation on Stock Exchange"

"Loans to Broker $167,000,000 Less" (p. 42) (Note: This article included: "As sterling and the franc continued to forge into new high ground for the year, reflecting the flight of European capital.")

"Utilities Report Increased Incomes" (p. 46)

On Saturday, October 19, the *Washington Post* (p. 13) headlined "20 Utility Stocks Hit New Low Mark" and ran an Associated Press story, "The utility shares again broke wide open and the general list came tumbling down almost half as far." The October 20 issue of the *Post* (p. 12) had another relevant Associated Press article: "The selling again concentrated today on the utilities, which were in general depressed to the lowest levels since early July."

An evaluation of the October 16 break in the *New York Times* on Sunday, October 20 (pp. 1 and 29), gave the following favorable factors:

1. stable business conditions
2. low money rates (5 percent)
3. good retail trade
4. revival of the bond market
5. buying power of investment trusts
6. largest short interest in history

The paper also described the following negative factors:

1. undigested investment trusts and new common stock shares
2. increase in broker loans
3. some high stock prices
4. lower agricultural prices
5. nervous market

The negative factors listed above were not very upsetting to an investor optimistic that the real economic boom (business prosperity) would continue.

The Monday, October 21, *Wall Street Journal* (p. 18) said, "Aside from a flood of unfavorable rumors, there were no tangible news developments to account for the weakness in the market." The paper did define a new term (p. 18) called "ex-public imagination." This was defined as public utility and airplane stocks (only with imagination can one justify the stock prices). The fact that the *Journal* implied that utility stocks were too high is important.

One aspect that was encouraging to the *Wall Street Journal* editor was the large short interest that had been built up in leading issues. These parties would have to buy when stocks started to raise in price. It was not noted that the margin buyers would have to sell if prices fell.

On Monday, October 21, the market went down significantly. The *New York Times* (October 22) identified the causes to be

1. margin sellers (buyers on margin being forced to sell)
2. foreign money liquidating
3. skillful short selling

The same October 22 *Times* issue (p. 24) carried an article about a talk by Irving Fisher: "Fisher says prices of stocks are low." Fisher also defended investment trusts as offering investors diversification, thus reduced risk. He was reminded that in May he had "pointed out that predicting the human behavior of the market was quite different from analyzing its economic soundness." Fisher admitted he was better with fundamentals than market psychology. The *Washington Post* (October 22, p. 13) had an article with the heading "Expect Bull Market." One can write an entire article on the bad forecasts made in 1929 on many different issues (not only forecasts applying to the stock market).

The news reported by the *Times* Wednesday, October 23, was mostly upbeat. One headline was "Mitchell decries decline in stocks," with the subhead, "Many issues are selling below true value." C. E. Mitchell was chairman of National City Bank and one of the most influential and respected New York bankers. On page sixteen was a small article, "Babson still pessimistic. Foresees new lows." The *Washington Post* had several cheerful articles: "Rallies in Market Offset Sales Loss" (p. 1) and "Swift Slap Dazes Shorts in Stocks" (p. 14). On Wednesday, October 23, the market crashed. The *Times* headline (October 24, p. 1) said, "Prices of Stocks Crash in Heavy Liquidation." The *Post* (p. 1) had "Huge Selling Wave Creates Near-Panic as Stocks Collapse." There were 2.6 million shares sold between 2 and 3 p.m. In a total market value of $87 billion the market declined $4 billion on October 23. The market had opened "calmly enough": "Many prices were higher" (p. 1). On page two the paper noted that there had been declines since September 1. If the events of the next day (Black Thursday) had not occurred, October 23 would have gone down in history as a major event.

The *Times* (October 24, p. 2) conjected that a bad snow and sleet storm in the Midwest had cut off communications and caused Midwest investors to sell rather than hold "blind." The *Times* (p. 38) lamented, "There was hardly a single item of news which might be construed as bearish."

On Wednesday, October 23, the Dow Jones Index dropped from 326.51 to 305.85, an impressive drop for one day of 6.3 percent. On Black Thursday the drop was to 299.47 or only 2.1 percent. However, the low for the day was 272.32, and this was a drop of 11.0 percent.

The index was 256.75 on Monday, October 28, and dropped to 212.33 on Black Tuesday, October 29—a drop of 17.3 percent. Black Tuesday wins the award for most dramatic 1929 price drop for a single day. The market closed October at a level of 273.51. It had opened in January at 300. Thus, the drop since January was only 8.8 percent. One reason the 1929 crash is considered such a disaster is that subsequent price decreases continued, with sporadic interruptions, until 1933.

THURSDAY, OCTOBER 24, 1929

Thursday, October 24 (Black Thursday), was a 12,894,650 share day (the previous record was 8,246,742 shares on March 26, 1929). The headline on page one of the *New York Times* (October 25) was "Treasury Officials Blame Speculation." Senator King gave his explanation (p. 3): "Gambling in stock has become a national disease." The *Times* (p. 2) reported that "Stocks opened moderately steady," but then the roof caved in.

The *Times* (p. 41) recalled that call money had been 20 percent in March and the price break in March was understandable. Call money on October 24 was available at 5 percent to 6 percent. There should not have been a crash. The Friday *Wall Street Journal* (October 25) gave the bankers credit for stopping the price decline with $1 billion of support.

On Thursday, October 24, the *Wall Street Journal* (p. 2) carried an article, "Fisher Discusses Stock Prices," in which he pointed to factors making for expansion in market volume and price. This was not the right lecture for Black Thursday.

Irving Fisher was also cited on October 24 (*Wall Street Journal*, p. 2) as opposing the capital gains tax as structured. He objected to only taxing realized gains since this prevented the tax aware person from selling stocks that went up too much. It is not clear whether Fisher would have favored taxing unrealized as well as realized gains, or whether he favored no taxation of such gains. It is clear that he was against the tax system that was in place (and that is still in place).

The *Washington Post* (October 26, p. 1) reported: "Market Drop Fails to Alarm Officials." The "officials" were all in Washington. The rest of the country was alarmed. On October 25 the market gained. President Hoover made a statement on Friday, October 25, regarding the excellent state of business but then added how building and construction had been adversely "affected by the high interest rates induced by stock speculation" (*New York Times*, October 26, p. 1). A *Times* editorial (p. 16) quoted Snowden's "orgy of speculation" comments made at the beginning of the month.

RELEVANT MARKET DATE: OCTOBER 29
(BLACK TUESDAY)

Paper of Saturday, October 26 (p. 1)

"Stocks Gain as Market is Steadied" (Note: Right-hand major headline.)

"President Hoover Issues a Statement of Reassurance on Continued Prosperity of Fundamental Business" (Note: The statement included, "The fundamental business of the country, that is production and distribution of commodities, is in a sound and prosperous basis.")

Finance Section (pp. 20–26)

"Stabilizing Efforts Evident in Securities"

"Decline Held Wholesome"

"Break Held Inevitable"

Paper of Sunday, October 27 (p. 1)

"Stocks Hold Firm in Normal Trading"

Finance Section (pp. N5–N16)

"Debacle Inevitable Wall St. Now Says"

"Business is Sound, Store Chains Say"

"Increase Expected in Steel's Profits"

"Conference Board Gives Data to Prove Business Sound and Gaining"

Paper of Monday, October 28 (p. 1)

"Roosevelt Medal Bestowed on Young" (Note: Owen D. Young was a leading statesman, potential presidential candidate, and ex-chairman of General Electric. Roosevelt was "Teddy.")

Finance Section (pp. 34–36)

A special report from Europe stated "Financial interests in London participated in the week's 'bear tactics' on Wall Street"

"Low Yield on Stock Drove Prices Down" (Berlin)

"Wall Street Crash Was Not Unexpected" (London)

Paper of Tuesday, October 29 (p. 1) Black Tuesday

"Stock Prices Slump $14,000,000,000" (Note: This was a right-hand major headline. The decline had been $4 billion on October 23 and $2 billion on October 24.)

"Bankers Mobilize for Buying Today" (Note: The Black Tuesday crash was to be reported the next day.)

Finance Section (p. 42)

"The decline was bigger than any bear or any group of bears"

Paper of Wednesday, October 30 (p. 1)

"Stocks Collapse in 16,410,035 Share Day" (Note: This was a right-hand major headline.)

"Reserve Board Finds Action Unnecessary"

"U.S. Steel to Pay $1 Extra Dividend"

"Investment Trusts Buy"

"240 Issues Lose $15,894,878,894 in Month"

The Sunday, October 27, edition of the *New York Times* had a two-column article, "Bay State Utilities Face Investigation." It implied that regulation was going to be less friendly towards utilities.

The Monday *Times* reported that the *Guaranty Survey* was critical of "mob psychology in exaggerated buying and selling" and "lays stock crash to gullible public."

Stocks again went down on Monday, October 28. There were 9,212,800 shares traded (three million in the final hour). The *Times* on Tuesday, October 29, again carried an article on the New York public utility investigating committee's criticism of the rate-making process. For October 29, "Black Tuesday," the headline was "Stocks Collapse in 16,410,030 Share Day" (October 30, p. 1). In the month of October stocks lost approximately .18 of the beginning of the month value. Twenty-nine public utilities (tabulated by the *New York Times*) lost $5.1 billion in the month, by far the largest loss of any of the industries listed by the *Times*. The value of the stocks of all public utilities went down by much more than this $5.1 billion.

The October 30 *New York Times* (p. 2) reported that margins were cut to 25 percent (the margins on some stocks had been as high as 75 percent), and that investment trusts were supporting the market (p. 7). On October 30 stocks did rally in heavy trading (10,727,320 shares traded), as they did on October 31. The *Wall Street Journal* (October 31, p. 1) had an article about John J. Rockefeller indicating that he was buying stock.

Paper of Thursday, October 31 (p. 1)

"Stocks Mount in Strong All-Day Rally"
"Rockefeller Buying Heartens Market"

Finance Section (p. 33)

"Returned Confidence"

On October 25 the *Wall Street Journal* (p. 1) gave credit to the bankers for preventing an even worse crash on October 24 "Bankers Halt Stock Debacle." Again on October 29 the *Journal* (p. 1) had the headline "Continued Operation of Bankers' Pool Prevents Repetition of Thursday's Hysteria." This paper was read on Black Tuesday as the market overwhelmed the bank's attempts at price stabilization. William Peter Hamilton, editor of the *Journal*, in a brilliant talk to the Bond Club of Washington D.C. (*Wall Street Journal*, October 19, p. 7), had anticipated the failure of the bank's efforts: "Wide Interest Makes Any General Manipulation Impossible." Even a $1 billion bank investment fund to stabilize the market could not succeed when the investors decided it was time to sell. Hamilton also predicted that "if activity in Wall Street greatly contracts then you can bet that within a few months the business of the country will contract also." His third insightful observation was that the broker loan information was being misinterpreted. This was a world class talk.

CONCLUSIONS

Aside from Snowden's orgy statement and the various articles dealing with public utility regulation, there are no obvious triggers to a crash in the newspapers of October. The several days with large declines seem to have generated other days with declines. This could be the result of margin selling as well as market overreaction. On the other hand, investors who sold and stayed out of the market until 1932 were the big winners.

CHAPTER 6

Investment Trusts and Margin Buying

Margin buying during the 1920s was not controlled by the government. It was controlled by brokers interested in their own financial well-being. Prior to October 1929 the average margin requirement was 50 percent of the stock price. On selected stocks it was as high as 75 percent. When the crash came no major brokerage firm was bankrupted, because the brokers managed their finances in a conservative manner. The fact that stock prices continued downward did result in three major brokerage firms going bankrupt in the first nine months of 1930. At the end of October margins were lowered to 25 percent. The level of the margin requirements at the beginning of October compared to the end of October implies that the broker community either thought some stock prices were too high on October 1 or too low on October 31.

In 1929 New York Stock Exchange member firms had 560,000 margin accounts out of 1,549,000 customers. Broker loans increased from $6,735 million to $8,549 million from January to September 1929. With a 50 percent margin the $1,814 million increase in broker loans would support $3,628 million of stock investment.

The market value of all stock securities (common and preferred stock) listed on the NYSE was $89.7 billion on September 1, 1929 (*Stock Exchange Practices*, 1934, p. 7). With a value of $67.5 billion in January, the market increased by approximately $22.2 billion during that eight-month period. Obviously, margin buying was not the only factor causing the upswing.

Using Wigmore's (1985, p. 641) $82.1 billion estimate of value of all common stock on the NYSE as of September 1, 1929, and the brokers' loans of $8.5 billion on October 1, 1929, the ratio of loans to market value is 10.4 percent. This ratio could be reduced by the fact that the broker loans would also be used to finance preferred stock, bonds, and stocks listed on other exchanges.

The *Wall Street Journal* (October 19, 1929, p. 9) reported that brokers' loans of members of the NYSE were only 9.82 percent of the market value of listed shares. In March 1928 it had been 10.25 percent. The point being made by the *Journal* was that brokers' loans were not excessively high compared to the recent past.

The broker loans reported by the NYSE increased from $6,735 million in January to $8,547 million in September. Of this amount $7,077 million was from New York banks and $1,472 million from "others" including foreign sources, up from $1,071 in January (*Federal Reserve Bulletin,* October 1930, p. 621). By December 1929 broker loans had contracted to $3,990 million, and loans from "others" had shrunk to $620 million.

The brokers' loans received a lot of attention in England, as they did in the United States. The *Financial Times* regularly reported the level and the changes in the amount. For example, the October 4 issue indicated that on October 3 broker loans reached a record high of $6.804 billion as money rates dropped from .075 to .06. By October 9 money rates had dropped further to below .06. Thus investors prior to October 24 had relatively easy access to funds at the lowest rate since July 1928.

The *Financial Times* (October 7, 1929, p. 3) reported that the president of the American Bankers Association was concerned about the level of credit for securities and had given a talk in which he stated, "Bankers are gravely alarmed over the mounting volume of credit being employed in carrying security loans, both by brokers and by individuals." The *Financial Times* was also concerned about the buying of investment trusts on margin and the lack of credit to support the bull market.

It is interesting that the amount of margin buying and the level of the loans to brokers were major concerns to the financial community in 1929, and in recent years these factors receive little or no attention in the financial press. Could they have been important in 1929 but not in subsequent years?

The conclusion is that the margin buying was a likely factor in causing stock prices to go up by increasing demand. There is no reason to conclude that margin buying triggered the October crash, but once the selling rush began, the calling of margin loans probably exacerbated the price declines. The buying of stock on margin was one more layer of leverage in a market that was already, in several segments, excessively levered.

Wigmore (1985) gives excellent statistics concerning the dividend yield and call loan costs (p. 572 and pp. 626–27). Given the low stock yields (3 percent) and the high costs of the loans to finance the stocks (5 to 14.4 percent), the investor buying on margin needed the expectation of stock price increases. This fact made the investors who bought on margin sensitive to any large selling activity and the possibility of stock prices not going up.

INVESTMENT TRUSTS

By 1929 investment trusts were very popular with investors. These trusts were the 1929 version of closed-end mutual funds. In recent years seasoned closed-end mutual funds sell at a discount to their fundamental value. The fundamental value is the sum of the market values of the fund's components (securities in the portfolio). In 1929 the investment trusts sold at a premium. Malkiel concludes (p. 51) that this "provides clinching evidence of wide-scale stock-market irrationality during the 1920s." However, Malkiel also notes (p. 442), "As of the mid-1990's, Berkshire Hathoway shares were selling at a hefty premium over the value of assets it owned." Warren Buffet is the guiding force behind Berkshire Hathaway's great success as an investor. If we were to conclude that rational investors would currently pay a premium for Warren Buffet's expertise, then we should reject a conclusion that the 1929 market was proven to be irrational.

We have current evidence that rational investors will pay a premium for what they consider to be superior money management skills.

It is true that to some extent investment trusts were misused by their organizers and managers. One scam was to "pyramid" (see the *Economist* of August 31, 1929). The trust would buy the stock of a subsidiary of the sponsor of the trust. It was hoped that the stock price of the subsidiary would increase, increasing the value of the trust but, more importantly, increasing the value of the sponsor's investment in the subsidiary. Obviously, there are limitations to the effectiveness of this type of strategy. If the subsidiary does not operate well the investment trust will suffer.

There were $1 billion of investment trusts sold in the first eight months of 1929 compared of $400 million in the entire year of 1928. The *Economist* reported that this was important (October 12, 1929, p. 665): "Much of the recent increase is to be accounted for by the extraordinary burst of investment trust financing." In September alone $643 million was invested in investment trusts (*Financial Times*, October 21, p. 3). While the two sets of numbers (from the *Economist* and the *Financial Times*) are not exactly comparable, both sets of numbers indicate that investment trusts had become very popular with investors by October 1929.

Wigmore (p. 44) shows the ratios of market price to book value for five investment trusts in 1929.

	Market Price Divided by Book Value
Goldman Sachs Trading	2.95
Lehman Corp.	1.49
Tri-Continental Corp.	3.56
United Corp.	2.05
United Founder	2.45

These ratios appear to be outrageous. But remember that book values were historic cost measures and not the market value of the trust's assets, thus the above table is meaningless. We do not know if these investment trusts were overvalued in 1929 since we do not know their net asset values. We do know that they dropped by over 30 percent in price from their highs in the crash. But the underlying stock prices also dropped by this magnitude.

The common stock of trusts that had used debt or preferred stock leverage were particularly vulnerable to the stock price declines. For example, the Goldman Sachs Trading Corporation was highly levered with preferred stock, and the value of its common stock fell from its high of $104 a share in 1929 to $1.75 in 1933. Many of the trusts were levered, but the leverage of choice was not debt but rather preferred stock.

In concept, investment trusts were a sensible investment alternative. They offered expert management and diversification. Unfortunately, in 1929 a diversification of stocks was not going to be a big help given the universal price decline. Irving Fisher on September 6, 1929, was quoted in the *New York Herald Tribune* as stating:

> The present high levels of stock prices and corresponding low levels of dividend returns are due largely to two factors. One, the anticipation of large dividend returns in the immediate future; and two, reduction of risk to investors largely brought about through investment diversification made possible for the investor by investment trusts.

If a researcher could find out the structure of a couple of dozen of the largest investment trusts as of September–October 1929 this would be extremely helpful. Seven important types of information that are not readily available but would be of interest are:

1. the percentage of the investment trust portfolios that were public utilities
2. the extent of diversification
3. the percentage of the portfolios that were NYSE firms
4. the investment turnover

5. the ratio of market price to net asset value at various points in time

6. the amount of debt and preferred stock leverage used

7. who bought the trusts and how long they held

The ideal information to establish whether market prices are excessively high compared to intrinsic values is to have both the prices and values at the same moment in time. For the normal financial security this is impossible since the intrinsic values are not objectively well defined. There are two exceptions. DeLong and Schleifer (1991) followed one path, very cleverly choosing to study closed-end mutual funds. Some of these funds are traded on the stock market, and the market values of the securities in the fund's portfolio provide a very reasonable estimate of the intrinsic value. DeLong and Schleifer state (p. 675):

> We use the difference between prices and net asset values of closed-end mutual funds at the end of the 1920s to estimate the degree to which the stock market was overvalued on the eve of the 1929 crash. We conclude that the stocks making up the S&P composite were priced at least 30 percent above fundamentals in late summer, 1929.

Unfortunately (p. 682), "portfolios were rarely published and net asset values rarely calculated." It was only after the crash that investment trusts started to reveal routinely their net asset value. In the third quarter of 1929 (p. 682), "Three types of event seemed to trigger a closed-end fund's publication of its portfolio." They were (1) listing on the New York Stock Exchange (most of the trusts were not listed); (2) start-up of a new closed-end fund (this stock price reflects marketing pressure); and (3) shares selling at a discount from net asset value (in September 1929 most trusts were not selling at a discount; the inclusion of any that were introduces a bias). After 1929 some trusts revealed 1929 net asset values. Thus DeLong and Schleifer lacked the amount and quality of information that would have allowed definite conclusions backed by hard evidence. In fact, if investors also lacked the information regarding the portfolio composition we would have to place investment trusts in a unique investment category where investment decisions were made without useful audited financial statements. If investors in the third quarter of 1929 did not know the current net asset value of investment trusts, this fact is significant.

The closed-end funds were an attractive vehicle to study since they were purchased by individual investors, not institutional buyers, thus broadly representing the stock market. Also, the market for investment trusts in 1929 was large and growing rapidly. In August and September alone over $1 billion of new funds were launched. DeLong and Schleifer found that the premiums of price over value were large (the median was about 50 percent in the third quarter of 1929, p. 678). But they worried about the validity of their study because funds were not selected randomly.

Another factor that would make generalizations from newly issued closed-end investment trusts difficult is that the funds were aggressively sold. There was frequently an organization fee of $X per share and an ongoing management fee (based on size and/or profits). In addition, the organizers received options to buy at net asset value. These were impressive incentives to form funds and sell the shares. They also were incentives to have successful funds.

DeLong and Schleifer had limited data (pp. 698–99). For example, for September 1929 there were two observations, for August 1929 there were five, and for July there were nine. The nine funds observed in July 1929 had the following premiums: 277 percent, 152 percent, 48 percent, 22 percent, 18 percent (2 times), 8 percent (3 times). Given that closed-end funds now tend to sell at a discount, the positive premiums are interesting. Given the conventional perspective in 1929 that financial experts could manage money better than the person not plugged into the street, it is not surprising that some investors were willing to pay for expertise and to buy shares in investment trusts. Thus a premium for investment trusts does not imply the same premium for other stocks.

The *Wall Street Journal* of October 1 (p. 1) took note of increasing investment trust prices: "The rapid advances in prices of some trust stocks to substantial premiums above liquidation values have injected a new complication into an already involved security market." But the *Journal* then added, however, that "management is the essence of investment trust valuation." Thus the premiums *might* be justified, if expert investment management was being bought.

There were very few news articles giving detailed information regarding investment trusts. The *New York Times* of October 17 (pp. 39 and 48) reported some facts regarding Capital Administration Company, Inc., a trust. On September 20 its net asset value was $42.08 per Class A share. The market price was $64⅞ with a high of $79⅛ and a low of $37½. The reason offered for the supply of information was a move by the trust from the Curb market to the NYSE.

On October 8 the *Wall Street Journal* (p. 1) reported the breakup value of Alleghany Corporation (a holding company whose prime asset was railroad stock) to be $30 on October 1 and market price on June 29 to be $31.81 and $35.53 on July 19. The book value was $18.32 on June 29. The analysis of holding companies and investment trusts is complicated by the fact that there are book value measures and net asset value measures, and we do not know the economic meaning of the book value measure being given. Obviously, neither $31.891 or $35.53 are material overvaluations of the $30 breakup value. The situation is further complicated by the fact that (p. 9): "all the holdings of Alleghany have not been disclosed." Thus even when we are given the breakup value it might understate the actual value to investors since some asset values are not disclosed.

The *Times* (October 1, p. 37) had an interesting tombstone for United States Electric Light & Power Shares announcing the sale of one million shares sold at $58. It listed the firm's portfolio of approximately sixty different securities, all public utilities. The amounts invested in each security were not revealed. The management fee and other expenses were not to exceed ½ of 1 percent. The dividend was defined to be 6 percent. The investors could put the securities back at net asset value less expenses. The banker who sponsored the tombstone was Calvin Bullock of Denver. He was also the

Table 6.1
The Incomes for Goldman
for Investment = $100,000,000

Assumed Investment Trust Income Before Goldman's Payment	Amount to Others	Amount to Goldman for Management
$8,000,000	$8,000,000	$0
10,000,000	8,000,000	2,000,000
15,000,000	12,000,000	3,000,000
20,000,000	16,000,000	4,000,000

president of International Superpower Corporation, another investment trust heavily invested in utilities.

THE GOLDMAN SACHS TRADING CORPORATION

The Goldman Sachs Trading Corporation has received a large amount of attention because of its large losses. In 1929 the stock had a high price of $350, and it fell to a price of $1.75 a share in 1933. In 1933 the corporation was dissolved. It was a major embarrassment to its parent.

The execution of the investment strategy turned out to be a disaster, but the underlying incentive plan for Goldman should have been attractive to an investor (*New York Times*, October 4, 1929, p. 8). The corporation "receives no compensation until the corporation earns during the year 8% on its capital." Also, Goldman made a $10 million investment, buying 10 percent of the shares at $100 a share (100,000 shares). We do not know if Goldman (the parent) bailed out early.

Goldman was to get .2 of the income if the income exceeded .08 of the book value, but only if the amount earned in a year was in excess of .08. Assume the total investment is $100 million. Table 6.1 shows the hypothetical payoffs to Goldman for different incomes.

The income distributions shown in Table 6.1 are not unfair, but they do offer a large incentive from the trading corporation to undertake investments with a large variance. The large variance investments combined with a large amount of leverage, a falling stock market, and slackening economic activity spelled disaster for the Goldman Sachs Trading Corporation.

The *Times* (October 4, p. 8) did describe one deal for the firm. Assumptions will be made for simplification, but the numbers to follow are reasonably accurate. Goldman Sachs Trading Corporation and Central States Electric formed Shenandoah Corporation and Blue Ridge Corporation. Shenandoah Corporation issued 6 percent convertible preference shares and common stock. Assume the preference shares were issued publicly and the common stock all went to its originators. The equity capital of Shenandoah was 34.6 percent preference stock. Shenandoah invested $62.50 million in Blue Ridge Corporation (see above). Blue Ridge Corporation issued $72 million of 6 percent convertible preference stock and $58 million of equity to the public. Blue Ridge Corporation invested $192.50 million in Central States Electric (see above) and other utilities, buying common stock.

To simplify the analysis, assume that Central States Electric received the entire $192.50 million from Blue Ridge and that Central States bought a $500 million real asset. Assume Central States used $307.50 million of debt. We now have the following balance sheets.

BALANCE SHEETS (IN MILLIONS)

BLUE RIDGE

Assets		Financing	
Common of Central	192.50	Convertible Preference	72.00
		Common-Public Issue	58.00
		Common-Shenandoah Issue	62.50
	192.50		192.50

SHENANDOAH

Assets		Financing	
Blue Ridge Stock	62.50	Preference	21.63
		Common (held by Goldman)	40.87
	62.50		62.50

CENTRAL

Assets		Financing	
Real Assets	500.00	Debt	307.50
		Common (held by Blue Ridge)	192.50
	500.00		500.00

Looking at the $500 million financing for Central on a consolidated basis we have

Debt of Central	$307.50	
Preference (Shenandoah)	21.63	(equal to $62.50 × .346)
Preference (Blue Ridge)	72.00	
Common	98.87	
	$500.00	

The asset seems to be financed with $98.87 equity, but this amount is misleading. The common may be divided:

Sold to Public (Blue Ridge)	$58.00
Supplied by Goldman Sachs Trading Corporation	40.87
Total Common	$98.87

But Goldman Sachs Trading Corporation would use leverage also. Assume the $40.87 million is split between debt and common. This would mean that Goldman could have $20.435 million of common and $20.435 of debt or preferred. If the investors had a 50 percent margin the common stock investors of Goldman would put up $10.2175 million to finance the $500 million asset purchased by Central States Electric. This is 2 percent Goldman investor equity. Obviously, the slightest adverse event would wipe out Goldman's equity in the $500 million asset. This is a very risky investment.

The October 4, 1929, issue of the *Wall Street Journal* had an extensive article on Goldman Sachs Trading Corporation. It had been operating for approximately a year and was reasonably profitable (paid a special $2 a share cash dividend). The article described the details of the acquisition by Goldman Sachs Trading Corporation of the more profitable Financial & Industrial Securities Corporation. The acquisition was implemented by the issuance of stock by Goldman Sachs Trading. The transaction was apparently structured to be fair to all parties.

Goldman Sachs Trading announced a policy of a 6 percent stock dividend per year. The *Wall Street Journal* article said, "Payment of dividends in stock is akin to paying dividends in cash and selling new shares to the stockholders." This, of course, is correct. However, it would also have been correct for the *Journal* to have added, "Payment of dividends in stock is also akin to the corporation retaining the earnings. The stock dividend itself does not affect shareholder wealth."

The directors of Goldman Sachs Trading Corporation had three members of the Sachs family and Waddill Catchings, Ralph Jones, Sidney J. Weinberg, W. S. Bowers, and Frank L. Taylor (*New York Times*, March 20, 1930, p. 38). A prospective investor would expect this team to do well.

CONGRESSIONAL INQUIRIES

The *Wall Street Journal* (October 8, 1929, p. 12) had an article titled "Inquiries Into Trust Holdings." Senator Couzens and Congressman McFadden announced that they wanted to conduct an investigation of the holdings of public utility shares by investment trust corporations. They were particularly interested in "the influence exerted over utilities" by the investment trusts. The article emphasized the antagonism of Washington toward Wall Street. Washington was clearly against the speculators, the New York banks, the investment trusts, the utility holding companies, and the New York Stock Exchange.

THE RUSH INTO MUTUAL FUNDS (1996)

The number of American households investing in mutual funds increased by 20 percent in 1995–1996 (*New York Times*, December 27, 1996, p. 1). The *Times* identified the problem with this increase as how the new investors in equity mutual funds will act if the market has a significant dip.

The amount invested in mutual funds increased from $866.5 billion in 1994 to $1,650 billion in 1996. The Investment Company Institute reported (*New York Times*, December 27, 1996, p. D-2) that 25 percent of the households they surveyed, that owned mutual funds, had pretax income of less than $35,000. This 25 percent did not have a large capacity for risk.

Thus the investment trusts of 1929 made a dramatic reappearance in 1995–1996 in the form of mutual funds. While the normal mutual fund is not levered, we can expect there to be exceptions. The stock market of 1929, before the crash, had many characteristics that were to be replicated in the markets of the future.

CONCLUSIONS

Investments trusts were important in October 1929 for several reasons. They competed for investment funds, thus drawing funds away from direct purchases of stock. To the extent the trusts invested in non-U.S. stocks, to a larger extent than individual investors it was a real reduction in demand for U.S. stocks.

Many of the trusts invested in public utility stocks with their relatively high dividends, thus inflating utility stock prices above their already high values. Also, the trusts added another level of leverage. More leverage was not needed and would turn out to be one of the accelerating factors of the crash.

One reason given for the crash was that the market was not able to digest the new issues of investment trust securities. This gave rise to the following story.

When J. P. Morgan admitted in 1903 that there were "undigested securities," Mr. James J. Hill "proposed a change in title to 'indigestible securities' " (*New York Times*, Monday, October 21, 1929, p. 38).

For the level of both margin buying and investment trusts, the most significant factor was that they both added layers of debt leverage. The leverage made the investor in the stock of investment trusts (especially the stock bought on margin) very vulnerable to any change in value of the underlying stock held by the trust.

CHAPTER 7

The Public Utility Sector

In addition to investment trusts, intrinsic values are reasonably well defined for regulated public utilities. The general rule currently applied by regulatory authorities is to allow utilities to earn a fair return on an allowed rate base. The fair return is defined to be equal to the utility's weighted average cost of capital. There are several reasons why a public utility can earn more or less than a fair return, but the target set by the regulatory authority is the weighted average cost of capital.

If a public utility has an allowed rate equity base of $X and is allowed to earn a return of r (rX in terms of dollars), after one year the firm's equity will be worth $X + rX$ or $(1+r)X$ with a present value of X. Remember that r is the return required by the market as well as the allowed return. The present value of the equity is equal to the present equity rate base, and the stock price should be equal to the equity rate base per share. Given the nature of public utility accounting, the book value of a utility's stock is approximately equal to the rate base. Thus the market value of a regulated public utility's stock should normally be reasonably close to the book value per share.

There can be time periods in which the utility can earn more (or less) than the allowed return. The reasons for this include regulatory practices that differ from the above, regulatory lag, changes in efficiency, changes in the weather, changes in the mix and number of customers, and prospects of deregulation. Also, the cost of equity may be different from the allowed return because of inaccurate (or incorrect) calculations or changing capital market conditions. While the stock price may differ from the book value, we would not expect the stock price to be very much different from the book value per share for very long if the regulatory process is as described. There should be a tendency for the stock price to revert to the book value for a public utility supplying an essential service where there is not effective competition and the rate commission is effectively allowing a fair return to be earned.

While the *Federal Power Commission v. Hope Natural Gas Company* case (1944) had not yet been decided, the *Bluefield Water Works v. P.S.C.* (1923) was a historical fact in 1929. Bluefield is one of the primary cases defining the regulatory process for determining a fair return on regulated assets. Thus even in 1929 there were limits of abnormal profits for a regulated firm.

In the year 1929 public utility stock prices were in excess of three times their book values. Sooner or later this price-book value relationship had to change unless the regulatory authorities were to continue to allow the utilities to earn large returns, or there existed a stream of investors who would buy the utility stocks, even at their high prices. The decision made by the Massachusetts Public Utility Commission in October 1929 applicable to the Edison Electric Illuminating Company of Boston and the stock market reaction to the decision made clear that neither of these improbable events was going to happen.

The October 19 issue of the *Commercial and Financial Chronicle* identified the main depressing influences on the market to be the indications of a recession in steel and the refusal of the Massachusetts Public Utility Commission to allow Edison Electric Illuminating Company of Boston to split its stock. The explanations offered by the Massachusetts Commission made the situation worse (the stock was not worth its price and the company's dividend would have to be reduced). The *Boston Daily Globe* featured this story on both October 12 and October 16.

The *Washington Post* (October 17, p. 1), in explaining the October 16 market declines (an Associated Press release), stated, "Professional traders also were obviously distressed at the printed remarks regarding inflation of power and light securities by the Massachusetts Public Utility Commission in its recent decision." This news release was widely circulated.

Consider the following values for the Dow Jones Stock Indices (month ends) for 1929 (Wigmore, 1985, p. 637):

		Industrials	Railroads	Utilities
1929	High	381.17	189.11	144.61
1929	Low	198.69	128.07	64.72

The highs were all in September and the lows in November 1929. The low prices as percentages of the high prices were:

Industrials	52%
Railroads	68%
Utilities	45%

The utilities dropped the furthest from the highs.

A comparison of the beginning of the year prices and the highest prices is also of interest.

	Industrials	Railroads	Utilities
January 1929	317.51	158.54	97.92
1929 high	381.17	189.11	144.61

The high prices as percentages of the January prices and the growth in the value percentages were:

	Ratio	Growth Percentage
Industrials	120%	20%

| Railroads | 119% | 19% |
| Utilities | 148% | 48% |

The growth in value for utilities during the first nine months of 1929 was over twice that of the other two groups.

The following high and low prices for 1929 for a typical set of public utilities and holding companies is illustrative of how severely public utility prices were hit by the October 1929 crash (*New York Times*, January 1, 1930). All the companies listed lost at least 50 percent of their market value.

Firm	High Price	Low Price	Low Price Divided by High Price
American Power & Light	175⅜	64¼	.37
American Superpower	71⅛	15	.21
Brooklyn Gas	248½	99	.44
Buffalo, Niagara & Eastern Power	128	61½	.48
Cities Service	68⅛	20	.29
Consolidated Gas Co. of N.Y.	183¼	80⅛	.44
Electric Bond and Share	189	50	.26
Long Island Lighting	91	40	.44
Niagara Hudson Power	30¾	11¼	.37
Transamerica	67⅜	20¼	.30

Picking on the utility segment of the market as the cause of a general break in the market in October may not be a sufficient explanation. But if we combine a besieged utility segment with levered investment trusts that had been purchased on margin, we have the beginning of a viable explanation for the crash. Remember, the investment trusts were heavily invested in utility stocks.

Public utilities helped fuel the large stock price increases from January to October 1929. The *Economist* (November 23, 1929, pp. 976–77) computed an index for thirty-four public utilities. The index was 200 at the beginning of the year, reached a maximum of 330 (a 65 percent increase) in September and then fell to 170 by the end of October (a 48 percent decrease).

The Dow-Jones Utility Index was 97.92 at the end of January and reached a high price of 144.61 in September. This was a 48 percent increase. Prices then fell to 88.27 in December, a 39 percent decrease.

While the exact measures of percentages of increase and decrease depend on the dates used and firms making up the index, there is no question that utility stock prices were explosive in 1929, both on the upswing and on the collapse.

THE MASSACHUSETTS TRIGGER

On August 2, 1929, the *New York Times* reported that the directors of the Edison Electric Illuminating Company of Boston had called a meeting of stockholders to obtain authorization for a stock split.

The Sunday, October 6, edition of the *New York Times* (pp. 9N and 14N) reported that the Federal Trade Commission "was ready to resume utility hearings."

On Saturday, October 12 (p. 27), the *Times* reported that the Massachusetts Public Utility Commission had rejected the stock split. The heading said: "Bars Stock Split by Boston Edison. Criticizes Dividend Policy. Holds Rates Should Not Be Raised Until Company Can Reduce Charge for Electricity." Boston Edison lost 15 points for the day even though the decision was released after the closing. The stock's high for the year was $440 and the stock had closed at $360 on Friday, October 11.

The Massachusetts Public Utility Commission (*New York Times*, October 12, p. 27) stated that it did not want to imply to investors that this was the "forerunner of substantial increases in dividends." They stated that the expectation of increased dividends was not justified. They offered "scathing criticisms of the company" (October 16, p. 42) and concluded (p. 42), "The public will take over such utilities as try to gobble up all profits available."

On October 15 the Boston City Council advised the mayor to initiate legislation for public ownership of Edison. On October 16 the department announced it would investigate the level of rates being charged by Edison, and on October 19 it set the dates for the inquiry.

On Tuesday, October 15, there was a discussion in the *New York Times* (p. 41) of the Massachusetts decision in the column "Topics in Wall Street." It "excited intense interest in public utility circles yesterday and undoubtedly had effect in depressing the issues of this group. . . . The decision is a far-reaching one and Wall Street expressed the greatest interest in what effect it will have, if any, upon commissions in other States."

Boston Edison had closed at 360 on Friday, October 11, losing 15 points before the rejection announcement was released. It dropped 61 points at its low on Monday (October 14), the first trading day, but closed at 328, a loss of 32 points.

On October 16, the *Times* (p. 42) reported that Governor Allen of Massachusetts was launching a full investigation of Boston Edison including "dividends, depreciation, and surplus."

One major factor that can be identified leading to the price break for public utilities was this ruling by the Massachusetts Public Utility Commission. The only specific action was that it refused to permit Edison Electric Illuminating Company of Boston to split its stock. Most finance academics would argue that the primary effects of a stock split would be to reduce the stock price by 50 percent and double the number of shares outstanding, thus leaving the total stock equity value unchanged. The event was not economically significant, and the stock split should have been easy to grant. But the commission made it clear it had additional messages to communicate. For example, the *Financial Times* (October 16, 1929, p. 7) reported that the commission advised the company to "reduce the selling price to the consumer." Boston was paying $.085 per kw hour and Cambridge only $.055. The *Boston Daily Globe* (October 16) reported on page one that a $600,000 rate cut was planned. There was also talk and news reports of public ownership and a shifting of control. The next day (October 17) the *Financial Times* (p. 3) re-

Table 7.1
Edison Electric Illuminating Company of Boston Trades Before the
Decision, October 1–11, 1929

Date (October 1929)	Volume (Shares)	High	Low	Close
1	34	365	365	365
2	109	365	360	360
3	68	365	360	360
4	63	362	360	360
5	33	360	360	360
6	Sunday			
7	155	360	358	360
8	535	395	360	390
9	76	390	380	380
10	207	380	375	375
11	247	375½	360	360

ported, "The worst pressure was against Public Utility shares," and the article heading read "Electric Issue Hard Hit."

EDISON ELECTRIC ILLUMINATING COMPANY OF BOSTON

During the first eleven days of October the Boston Edison stock closed at between 360 and 390. The largest amount of trading was 535 shares on October 8 (see Table 7.1). Table 7.2 shows the trading for the next eleven days. The high for the Monday after the news of the commission's decision was 30 points lower than Friday's close. During the day the stock went as low as 299 (a 61 point day) and closed at 328. On October 23 it closed at 280.

Table 7.3 shows the stock's performance through Black Thursday (October 24) and Black Tuesday (October 29). The stock fell from $280 on October 23 to $250 at the end of the month (the low for the month was $240). The total price drop from the October 1 price

Table 7.2
Trades After the Decision, October 12–23, 1929

Date (October 1929)	Volume (Shares)	High	Low	Close
12	A Holiday			
13	Sunday			
14	7,850	330	299	328
15	1,982	324	310½	310½
16	2,241	309	290	290
17	1,265	304	290	303
18	617	303	300	300
19	289	299½	290	290
20	Sunday			
21	896	295	285	293
22	226	298	292	296
23	624	293	280	280

of 365 to 250 on October 30 was a 31.5 percent drop. For October 1 to October 23 there was a 23.3 percent drop. Thus the largest amount of Boston Edison's price decline preceded the market crash (there was a $115 price drop of which $85 or 74 percent took place before the crash).

There is no question that the stock price of Edison Electric Illuminating Company of Boston was greatly affected by the Massachusett's commission's decision and pronouncements.

Other public utilities were also affected. For example, from October 10 to October 16 American Power & Light fell 14.7 percent, American Superpower fell 12.0 percent, and Electric Bond and Share fell 12.9 percent. Remember that Black Thursday was still a week away from the closing prices on October 16.

The October 17 the *Wall Street Journal* (p. 1) identified the October 16 price drop as a break in utility stock prices. "The price structure of several leading active utility issues crumbled under a combination of professional attack and liquidation yesterday." The

Table 7.3
Trades During the Crash, October 24–31, 1929

Date (October 1929)	Volume (Shares)	High	Low	Close
24	1,290	285	276	273
25	365	280	275	275
26	232	280	275½	278
27	Sunday			
28	473	278	240	240
29	1,840	250	240	250
30	1,547	250	240	250

article then referred to the decision by the Massachusetts commission: "It was pointed out in some quarters that the stand taken by the commission held possibilities of changing the public attitude towards the utility shares, which it has been recognized have been discounting prospects to an unusual degree." The article concluded that the events would harm utility expansion plans. On October 18 there was an editorial in the *Wall Street Journal* (p. 1) on the unfairness of the Massachusetts ruling, especially the commission's criticism of the utility's depreciation accruals (the *Journal* pointed out they exceeded the requirements of the commission).

OTHER REGULATORY FACTORS

Massachusetts was not alone in challenging the utilities. The Federal Trade Commission, New York City, and New York State were all challenging the status of public utility regulation. The New York governor (F. D. Roosevelt) appointed a committee on October 8 to investigate the regulation of public utilities in the state. The committee stated (*New York Times*, October 17, p. 18), "This inquiry is likely to have far-reaching effects and may lead to similar action in other States." Both the October 17 and October 19 issues of the *Times* carried articles regarding the New York investigative committee. Professor James C. Bonbright of Columbia University, a

Roosevelt appointee, described the present process as a "vicious system" (October 19, p. 21) and said that consumers were ignored. The chairman of the Public Service Commission, testifying before the committee, wanted more control over utility holding companies, especially management fees and other transfers. The Tuesday, October 22, *Wall Street Journal* (p. 1) was highly critical of Bonbright's jump to a conclusion with his "vicious system" comment after the study had barely started and his "impatience to arrive at predetermined results." On page three it was noted that "Utilities Sell 24 Times Net." This was down from 35 in July and August. It implies that prices of public utility stocks had fallen 31 percent.

The New York committee also noted the increasing importance of investment trusts: "Mention of the influence of the investment trust on utility securities is too important for this committee to ignore" (*New York Times*, October 17, p. 18). They conjected that the trusts had $3.5 billion to invest, and "their influence has become very important" (p. 18).

In New York City, Mayor Jimmy Walker was fighting the accusation of graft charges with statements that his administration would fight aggressively against utility rate increases, thus "proving" that he had not accepted bribes (*New York Times*, October 23).

It is reasonable to conclude that the October 16 break was related to the news from Washington, Massachusetts, and New York concerning public utility regulation, though the head of a New York Stock Exchange house had a more simple explanation: "More sellers than buyers" (*New York Times*, October 17, p. 38).

On October 17 *New York Times* (p. 18) reported that the Committee on Public Service Securities of the Investment Banking Association warned against "speculative and uninformed buying." The committee published a report in which it "asks care in buying shares in utilities."

On Black Thursday, October 24, the market panic accelerated. Volume was 12 million shares on the NYSE and 6 million shares on the Curb. The market dropped from 305.87 to 272.32 (a 34-point drop, or 11 percent) and closed at 299.47. The declines were "led" by the motor stocks and public utilities.

THE PRICES OF UTILITY STOCKS

At their September price height, public utilities were very aggressively priced. Consider the following measures (Wigmore, 1985, p. 39) for five operating utilities that were typical:

1929 Price-earnings Ratio

	High Price for Year	Market Price/ Book Value
Commonwealth Edison	35	3.31
Consolidated Gas Co. of N.Y.	39	3.34
Detroit Edison	35	3.06
Pacific Gas & Electric	28	3.30
Public Service of N.J.	35	3.14

Public utility holding companies had even larger price-earnings ratios and market to book value ratios than did operating utilities.

As of September 1, 1929, all common stock listed on the New York Stock Exchange had a value of $82.1 billion. The utilities industry represented $14.8 billion of value and utilities were 14.8/82.1 = 18 percent of the value of the outstanding shares on the NYSE. Utilities were a significant fraction of the stock market.

Given that the above firms were all regulated utilities and if they were allowed to earn no more than a "fair return," we would have to conclude that public utilities in the beginning of October 1929 were overpriced. A public utility allowed to earn a fair return should sell approximately at its book value (rate base) if the market expects it to earn a fair return. When a public utility is selling at over three times book value the investors are expecting the firm to earn massive abnormal profits, inconsistent with logical regulatory policies and theories. The public utilities in September 1929 were very aggressively priced, and a prudent investor would have a difficult time justifying an investment in these firms at the September 1929 prices, given the announcements from the regulatory authorities and political figures in October 1929.

THE PUBLIC UTILITY MULTIPLIERS

Public utilities were a very important segment of the stock market, and even more important, any change in public utility stock values resulted in larger changes in equity wealth of investors. In 1929 there were three important multipliers that meant that any change in a public utility's underlying value would result in a larger value change in the market and in the investor's value. Consider the following hypothetical, but representative, values for a public utility:

Book value per share for a utility	$ 50.00
Market price per share of utility	162.50*
Market price of investment trust holding stock (assuming a 100% premium over market value)	325.00

*Based on a price to book value ratio of 3.25 (Wigmore, p. 39).

If we were to eliminate both the utility's $112.50 market price premium over book value, and the investment trust's premium over market price of the stock, the market price of the investment trust would be $50 without a price premium. The loss in market value of the stock of the investment trust and the utility would be $387.50 (with no premiums). The $387.50 is equal to the $112.50 loss in underlying stock value and the $275 reduction in investment trust stock value.

The public utility holding companies were even more vulnerable to a stock price change since their ratio of price to book value averaged 4.44 (Wigmore, p. 43). Assume the following situation:

Book value per share for a holding company	$ 50.00
Market price per share (4.44 times book value) for the holding company stock	222.00

Market price of investment trust holding stock   444.00
(assuming 100% premium over market
value)

If we were to eliminate the two premiums over book value, the loss in market values of the underlying stock and the investment trust stock would be $566. This assumes the trust lost its premium and traded at liquidation (net asset) value.

For simplicity we assumed the trust held all the holding company stock. The effects shown would be reduced if the trust held only a fraction of the stock. However, we also assumed that no debt or margin was used to finance the investment. Assume the individual investors invested only $222 of their money and borrowed $222 to buy the investment trust stock costing $444. If the holding company stock went down from $222 to $111 (selling for 2.22 times book) and the trust still sold at a 100 percent premium, the trust would sell at $222 and the investors would have lost 100 percent of their investment since the investors have a $222 asset and owe $222. At a price of $111 the holding company would still be selling at an inflated 2.22 times book value. The vulnerability of the margin investor buying a trust stock where the asset is utility holding company stock is obvious. Remember, the trust can also be highly levered (primarily by the use of preferred stock).

The impact on the several layers of leverage was enormous. Consider the following example. Assume that a utility with assets of $2 million has $1 million of stock equity and $1 million of debt. The $1 million of stock is owned by a holding company with $700,000 of debt and $300,000 of stock. The $300,000 of holding company stock is held by an investment trust financed with $100,000 of common and $200,000 of preferred stock. The $100,000 of common is financed by the individual investor with $50,000 of margin debt and $50,000 of investor equity funds. Thus $50,000 of investor equity funds is supporting $2 million of operating assets owned by a public utility.

If the $1 million of utility stock decreases $100,000 in value to $900,000, the value of the holding company's stock becomes

$200,000 since there is $700,000 of debt. The investment trust's common stock's value is reduced to zero (the $200,000 holding company stock value all goes to the preferred stock). Only a very small change in the public utility's stock value is required to wipe out the investor in the investment trust if one considers all the layers of leverage. In this example, a 5 percent ($100,000) reduction in the utility's asset results in the equity investors losing 100 percent of their investment.

It was not any one layer of leverage that was excessive but rather the cumulative effect of the leverages at all levels. In 1929 there were frequently several layers of holding companies and investment trusts, each layer introducing more leverage. Investment trusts liked to invest in public utilities since utilities paid relatively high cash dividends, and enabled the investment trusts to pay dividends.

A DIFFERENT INTERPRETATION

One conclusion to this point could be that public utility stocks were overpriced prior to October 1929. This implies a lack of rationality on the part of the investors. Let us consider a different interpretation.

As long as the regulatory commissions allowed stock investors to earn abnormal returns, it was rational for the investors to pay more than book value for the stock of the utilities. As soon as there were indications in Massachusetts, New York, and Washington that the regulatory commissions in the future would allow only a fair return on the capital invested in the utility, the stock prices had to fall to be closer to book value. Actually, by 1933 the utility stock prices fell to far below book value, reflecting both an overreaction on the part of the investing community to the events of the fall of 1929 and a changed economic environment.

Some of the drop in utility prices occurred in 1932 and 1933 when it was obvious that the new Democratic administration in Washington was going to be unfriendly to utility investors and would protect the interests of consumers with a great deal of zeal.

THE LARGE AMOUNT OF LEVERAGE

The amount of leverage (both debt and preferred stock) used in the utility sector was enormous. Assume that a utility purchases an asset that costs $1 million and that asset is financed with 40 percent stock ($400,000) and 60 percent debt. A utility holding company owns the utility stock and is also financed with 40 percent stock ($160,000). An investment trust owns the holding company's stock and is financed with 40 percent stock ($64,000). An investor buys the investment trust's common stock using 50 percent margin and investing $32,000 in the stock. Thus the $1 million utility asset is financed with $32,000 of equity capital.

When the large amount of leverage is combined with the inflated prices of the public utility stocks, the holding company stocks, and the investment trusts, the problem is even more dramatic. Continuing the above example, assume that the $1 million asset is again financed with $600,000 of debt and $400,000 common stock, but the common stock has a $1.2 million market value. The utility holding company has $720,000 of debt and $480,000 of common. The investment trust has $288,000 of debt and $192,000 of common stock. The investor $96,000 of margin debt. The $1 million asset is supporting $1,704,000 of debt. The investor's $96,000 of equity is very much in jeopardy.

On December 27, 1929, the *Times* (p. 32) had all listed stocks at $63.6 billion and gas and electric operating companies at $3.83 billion and gas and electric holding companies at $3.58 billion (as of December 1929). Together these utilities were then 11.7 percent of the stock market, and the market value of the holding company stocks was approximately as large in total as that of the operating companies.

A tombstone published in the *Wall Street Journal* (October 1, 1929, p. 17) advertised the issuance of one million shares of stock at $58 a share for the United States Electric Light & Power. The tombstone showed that this investment trust owned seventy-four different utility securities. While this trust had wide diversification within the one industry, the investors had a large amount of risk.

THE BANKS

The bank stocks were also alleged to be highly overpriced. Were the banks overvalued in 1929? Consider the nine banks reviewed by Wigmore (1985, p. 49). The highest 1929 market price of National City Bank was 13 times book value and the other money center banks were also selling at a large multiple of book value (the lowest was over 3 times book). Using the high 1929 prices the dividend yields were all less than 2 percent and the price-earnings ratios were all in excess of 30 (National City's price-earnings ratio was 120). A case can be made that the bank stocks were too high. But recognizing that in 1929 the books were a mixture of commercial banks and investment banks and their growth potentials were very large, it is difficult to reach a definite conclusion. The primary factor that gives one pause is the investment record of the two primary New York bank executives in 1929, Charles E. Mitchell and Albert Wiggin. Mitchell, the president of the bank, bought heavily of National City Bank stock in 1929 during the crash and already had significant holdings of his bank's stock. Mitchell clearly thought his bank deserved its price.

Wiggin, chairman of Chase National Bank, sold some of his bank's stock from September through November 1929, but after the October crash bought heavily long before the stock reached its nadir. By the end of 1933 the Wiggin family owned 194,000 shares. So there is some evidence that these two significant insiders did not think the stocks of their banks were terribly overpriced in 1929, though it can be argued reasonably that Wiggin was becoming nervous about the level of the market or the level of Chase's stock in September 1929—thus his sale of 42,506 shares. After utilities and investment trusts, bank stocks are the next candidate for being labeled "overpriced." They were not undervalued, using conventional financial measures.

CONCLUSIONS

Assuming they were to be allowed to earn only a fair return, utility common stocks were overvalued at the beginning of October 1929.

The Dow-Jones Utility Index (Wigmore, 1985, p. 637) was 97.92 in January and had gone up to 139.61 at the end of September (a 43 percent increase). Neither the earnings or the prospective regulated earnings (represented by the book value per share) justified this price increase, unless the regulatory commissions were very friendly to utilities. Compounding the problem was the leverage used by the utilities, the holding companies, the investment trusts, and the investors. A small change in market price of a utility stock would trigger a massive change in the value of the equity securities held by individual investors. In October investors were bombarded with news reports indicating an adverse change in the regulatory environment, and the prices of utility stock fell like a rock. The value of the utility holding companies and the investment trusts (heavily invested in utility stocks) was also hit very hard.

CHAPTER 8

The Accused

It would have been satisfying to those who suffered losses if one could have named and punished the persons responsible for the 1929 stock market crash. In the 1930s attempts were made to do this. There were four important parties attacked by the powers in Washington. These were:

Charles E. Mitchell, chairman of National City Bank

Albert H. Wiggin, chairman of Chase National Bank

Sam Insull, head of a public utility empire

J. P. Morgan & Co., a major investment banking and banking firm

The J. P. Morgan & Co. investigation by the U.S. Senate captured headlines on the front page of the *New York Times* for several weeks in 1933 because the firm's client list included important names and little was known prior to that time about the inner workings of Morgan. But the investigation never uncovered wrongdoing. The most revealing fact uncovered was that the more profitable customers were treated favorably. Edmund Platt, the former vice governor of the Federal Reserve Board, called the investigation and treatment of the Morgan people a disgrace to the Senate.

This chapter will focus on Mitchell, Wiggin, and Insull. These are the three names that one finds in Galbraith (1961) and other similar exposés of the "evil excesses" of Wall Street in 1929.

In 1933 the U.S. Senate Committee on Banking and Currency held hearings on stock exchange practices. Two of the major targets were Charles E. Mitchell and Albert Henry Wiggin. Charles E. Mitchell was the president of the National City Bank in 1929. Ferdinand Pecora was the counsel of the subcommittee conducting the hearings and later the author of a book (1939). In order to better understand the Mitchell case it is necessary to review briefly events of March 1929 when the crash did not occur.

CHARLES E. MITCHELL

On March 25 and March 26, 1929, stock prices were down drastically and call money had risen to 20 percent. On March 26 the market dropped 9.6 percent on a volume of 8,246,000 shares (the volume was much greater than the six million shares traded the day before and the day after). Starting in February, the Federal Reserve had discouraged its member banks from making loans to finance securities. It looked as if a crash was in process. On March 26 Mitchell's National City Bank stepped in and made loans available to brokers. The bank announced it was ready to lend $25 million on the call market. The loans were to be made at rates of 16 percent and higher.

A newspaper carried an article that quoted Mitchell as telling the Federal Reserve Board to "go to hell." Mitchell later denied the quote, but Congress believed it. Senator Carter Glass blasted Mitchell: "He avows his superior obligation to a frantic stock market over the obligations of his oath as a director of the New York Federal Reserve Bank" (*New York Times*, March 29, 1929, p. 1). Senator Glass carried this view of Mitchell well into the thirties.

President Hoover also disapproved of Mitchell's actions, later writing that Mitchell "issues a defiance and engages in an attempt to mitigate the policy of the Federal Reserve Board" when the board was seeking to "abate" the "menacing spectacle of excessive stock gambling" (Hoover, 1952, pp. 18–19).

The subcommittee of the U.S. Senate Committee on Banking and Currency studying stock exchange practices in its investigation attacked Mitchell's March 1929 actions in helping prevent a crash at that time. For example, Senator Brookhart stated to Mitchell, "If you had let it collapse in March that would have saved hundreds of thousands of dollars to people who invested later on." Thus Mitchell, who helped avert a selling panic in March, was blamed for the severity of the October crash (*Stock Exchange Practices*, 1933).

Failing to find any indictable offense for his March 1929 actions, the subcommittee sought to find evidence of stock manipulation by Mitchell. They would like to have shown that Mitchell profited from the tremendous run-up in price of National City Bank's stock. For example, the investigating committee's counsel Ferdinand Pecora (Pecora, 1939, pp. 110–11) writes, "National City Bank stock, which had a par value of $100, was pushed up and up until it reached dizzy heights." The reference to par value indicates that Pecora was not a student of finance (he was legal counsel of the subcommittee). Pecora does not reveal who pushed up the stock price. He also writes, "For the proud privilege of owning these shares, worth $140,000,000 at their highest book value, the public paid the stupendous sum of $650,000,000." The reference to the book value of a bank stock with the bank heavily engaged in investment banking activities does not enhance our confidence in Pecora's financial sophistication. The implication was that Mitchell "pushed up" the price of the stock, and the market value for 1,300,000 shares of $650,000,000 ($500 a share) was in some sense morally or criminally wrong. The stock reached a high of $580 in September 1929 before it began its slide.

Senator Brookhart questioned Mitchell about his National City Bank stock transactions. Unfortunately for Brookhart, Mitchell responded to the question "In what years did you buy?" with "I bought the largest amount of stock in 1929." In answer to "Before or after the collapse?" Mitchell responded "In the midst of the panic."

Senator Brookhart also found out that Mitchell bought at $375 a share (the stock went down to $16 in 1933). Pecora asked whether Mitchell had sold any substantial portion of his holdings of National City Bank stock in 1929. Mitchell had purchased 28,300 shares in October 1929 and sold 10,000 shares, leaving him a net ownership of 53,300 shares. In 1933 when the stock fell to $16 he held more than 53,300 shares.

Rather than proving that Mitchell was manipulating the market, Brookhart and Pecora extracted from his testimony that he was the number one victim of the stock market increase (buying at $375 and higher) and then the decrease in National City Bank stock. It becomes obvious to an impartial observer that Mitchell deserved praise for the ethics of his market transactions in his bank's stock, not censure.

The testimony at the hearing then shifted to a topic where Mitchell was more vulnerable, the sale of stock to his wife for tax purposes. Here the government had a worthwhile target, but they chose the wrong battle, a criminal trial.

Galbraith (1961, p. 155) writes, "By comparison with the National City the troubles of the Chase were slight." But there were no troubles at National City Bank. There was a disagreement with regard to Mitchell's tax return but not a problem that had to be resolved in federal court in a criminal case.

The counsel for the subcommittee, Ferdinand Pecora, was born in Sicily and was brought to the United States at age five. In 1933 he was fifty-one years old. His full time college education consisted of one year at St. Stephens College. He then went to work at a law office to help support six young siblings, while attending law school part time. In 1909 he was accepted to the bar at age twenty-seven. He had a fine record of public service working as a district attorney and then left for private practice. In January 1933 he was approached by Chairman Norbeck to act as counsel for the Senate committee. The salary was $255 a month (a good salary but not comparable to the wages of the people he was to question). In May 28, 1933, there were published reports ("innuendoes") of "Slurs on Pecora" but nothing of significance was ever revealed. It would appear that someone did not like him. This list would soon get larger.

It is interesting that three of the major characters in this drama had lived the American dream up to 1929. Wiggin was chairman of a bank that was soon to be the world's largest bank. He went to work as a clerk on graduating from high school. Sam Insull controlled a $3 billion public utility empire. He went to work as an apprentice clerk at age fourteen in England. It is noted above that the prosecutor, Pecora, came to the United States at age five and at age fifteen had to stop his full-time education. If only prohibition had not existed and the three of them could have gone to a pub for a couple of beers rather than perform their sad dramas in court and public inquiries.

On January 30, 1933 (*New York Times,* January 31, 1933, p. 11), Ferdinand Pecora, counsel of the Senate subcommittee of the Committee on Banking and Currency, subpoenaed Charles E. Mitchell to testify. On February 2 the *Times* (p. 25) reported that the Senate inquiry aimed to show that the banks caused the boom and that the marketing of their own stock contributed to inflated stock prices. Mitchell was particularly at fault since he "took a go-to-hell" attitude towards the Federal Reserve Board in March 1929 when the board attempted to restrain the boom. The subcommittee's chairman, Senator Norbeck, stated, "Some of the large banks were highly responsible for the wild stock market boom" and "It was just a polite way of robbing the public."

Mitchell's testimony led to the page one headlines (*Times*) on February 22, 1933: "Mitchell Avoided Income Tax in 1929 By $2,800,000 Loss" and "Got $3,500,000 in 3 Years." The $3,500,000 were bonuses received by Mitchell from the bank. Senator Couzens (p. 12) described Mitchell as "a better salesman than a financier" without implying that he was a bad financier but acknowledging his appealing personality.

The February 23, 1933, *Times* (p. 1) revealed that "National City Lent $2,400,000 to Save Stock of Officers. Bank Charged Them No Interest. Sold Out The Customers." There were one hundred officers so protected but not Mitchell. He borrowed from J. P. Mor-

gan & Co. The same paper (p. 27) had an article in which Senator
Wheeler of Montana "Assails Mitchell."

On February 25 there was another page one headline, "Federal
Inquiry on National City and Insull Starts. Law Violations Sought."
Given the 1929 stock market crash, somebody had to be guilty of
something. On February 27 (again p. 1), "Mitchell Offers to Quit
National City Bank. Letter of Resignation Up For Action Today."
The next day the resignation of Mitchell was accepted by the bank's
board. President-elect Franklin Roosevelt advised the banker to re-
tire. A *Times* editorial (p. 18) with the heading "Better Banking"
said the "resignation was inevitable." Thus with no crime, even
hinted at, other than differences of opinion regarding Mitchell's tax
bill, Mitchell was driven from his position by vague accusations that
he and his bank caused the stock market boom.

Pecora released a statement to the press that "any public misun-
derstanding created by Mr. Mitchell's testimony was due to Mr.
Mitchell himself." Next Pecora went after the marketing by National
City Bank of $90 million of Peru bonds issued in 1927 and 1928.
National City had a net of $687,000 on the transactions, and in
1931 the investors lost when the bonds stopped paying interest. The
accusation was that the bank had acted contrary to advice given by
South American experts against participation in Peruvian bond flo-
tations.

In 1921 the vice president in charge of the Lima branch (Claud
W. Calvin) of National City Bank described the Peruvian financial
situation as being "positively distressing" and said the country's
Treasury was "flat on its back." In May 1923 National City rejected
participating in a $6 million Peruvian bond issue proposal because
there was too much risk. In July 1923 the bank again rejected a
Peruvian bond proposal because of risk.

In 1925 Mr. Calvin (see above) sent a letter to the bank's New
York office saying that there was so much progress under President
Leguia that he felt the underwriting should be reconsidered (*Times*,
February 28, 1933, p. 6). National waited two years before it joined
the Seligman syndicate. The factors that swung the decision were

Calvin's report and the fact that the bonds were to be secured by a tobacco monopoly.

In 1927 National City Bank agreed to join a syndicate to market a $15 million issue (National's share was $5 million). The syndicate was headed and managed by J. W. Seligman & Co. The stated purpose of the issue was to refinance outstanding bonds (these bonds had not been marketed by National). Thus, if the new bonds had not been issued the holders of the old bonds would have suffered an equivalent loss.

One factor cited by Pecora as evidence of excessive risk was that the Peruvian government budget had only been balanced in three of the ten years from 1914 to 1925! What would Pecora have said about the last forty years of United States federal government budgets?

Peru's president wanted a consolidation of the country's external debt and he promised the underwriters a stabilized currency and a balanced budget. In 1931 there was political unrest and a major revolution in Peru, and the Peruvian bonds failed to pay interest in May 1931. In 1933 Peru was at war with Colombia. The bonds went down further in price.

National City admitted to "an honest mistake." The implication that National City Bank (and Mitchell) were culpable is unfair. It was not unreasonable for National City to market Peruvian bonds in 1927 and 1928. If there were criticisms they should have been made in 1927 and 1928 at the time of the deals rather than in 1933 based on the wisdom offered by hindsight. There is no question that the bonds were risky at the time of issue, but an optimist could rationally buy the bonds based on the reports that were available.

The *Times*, October 9, 1929 (p. 53), had an article with the heading "Loan Record Made by Latin America." The total borrowings by Latin American countries in 1928 were $344,598,000 of which $106,400,000 was refunding of loans held by Americans. The article cited the Bolivia-Paraguay boundary dispute and the credit situation in Brazil and stated, "These developments detracted somewhat from the year's generally favorable trend." As part of the favorable trend it said, "A law was enacted in Peru creating the Mortgage Bank of Peru."

On March 3, 1933 (p. 25), the *Times* reported "Profit in Mergers." A merger leading to the combination of several airplane manufacturers into Boeing Air led to a National City Bank fee of $2,499,250. The common stock was issued to friends and officers of the National City Bank. Mitchell indicated that the offering was "too speculative" for a public offering. If the stock had been offered to the public and had gone down, the hearings would have been more productive. The hearings did bring out that in violation of Federal Law, National City Bank did hold bank stock for a short period of time (p. 25 of the March 3 *Times*).

In his inaugural address Roosevelt stated (p. 1, March 5, 1933), "Practices of the unscrupulous money changers stand indicted in the court of public opinion, rejected by the hearts and minds of men." He did not identify who was "unscrupulous," but Mitchell was the man making the front page of the *Times* during the moment of Roosevelt's taking office.

President Roosevelt, newly inaugurated, gave the stock practices hearings new vigor with a statement upholding the banking inquiry with an objective to eliminate "bad banking practices."

On March 17 the *Times* had an article dealing with a report to the Senate Committee on Banking and Currency. The report concluded that pools can control prices and that one of the techniques used by speculators was "selling against the box."[1] The report said corrective legislation was required.

The *Times* (March 18, 1933, p. 1) reported that Attorney General Cummings was "Hunting Law Violations." President Roosevelt was quoted as asking him "vigorously to prosecute any violation of the law." The next day's headline (p. 1): "Mitchell Will Face Grand Jury Inquiry." The accusation was that he illegally evaded an income tax payment in 1929.

In 1929 Mitchell purchased 28,300 shares of the National City Bank stock at prices of approximately $369 a share (*Times*, March

---

[1]The term "selling against the box" refers to a process in which an investor owning stock, wanting to "protect" a gain, sells the stock short. If the stock goes down, there is no net loss. The process is a legitimate process (not necessarily advisable).

19, 1933, p. 1). His motivation was either to support the stock price (his position) or to take advantage of the drop in price (from its high of above $580). In 1929 he "sold" 18,300 shares to his wife at a price of $212, thus had a loss of $2,872,306 that he then took as a deduction on his 1929 tax return. Since he reported a gain on sale of other stock of $1,388,238, the $1,484,068 net loss resulted in a deduction against salary and other incomes.

Three days after the grand jury inquiry was announced there was the headline "Mitchell Arrested as Tax Evader" (*Times*, March 22, 1933, p. 1). The government wanted a $657,152 payment. An interesting sidelight is that the Federal Marshall (Mulligan) had to borrow a car from his brother to drive the arrested Mitchell to the court house. Bail was set at $10,000. The assistant U.S. district attorney directing the arrest was Thomas E. Dewey.

On March 23, 1933 (p. 1), the headline was "Mitchell Evidence Goes to Grand Jury" and on March 25 (p. 1) "Mitchell Indicted." On April 14 the indictment was changed to include Mitchell's 1930 tax. On April 22 there was a second change. The tax total was reduced by $40,000 (the government had calculated wrong). On April 26 a third change was made. The government claimed Mitchell had $666,666 of additional income (Mitchell said he owed the money, thus it was a loan and not income).

In a speech extolling the virtues of the new securities law Chairman Sam Rayburn of the Commerce Committee of the House said "Since the World War some $50,000,000,000 in new securities have been floated in the United States and fully $25,000,000,000 have proved to be worthless." This unsubstantiated comment reflected the mood of Congress. There was not a friendly feeling for Wall Street or bankers in Washington.

On May 12 (p. 1) the trial began. Max D. Steuer, Mitchell's lawyer, described Mitchell as a "ruined patriot" and noted that he "lost $25,000,000 protecting bank and country" (May 17, p. 1). Mitchell owned 53,300 shares of bank stock at the end of 1929. A price drop of $469 would lead to a $25 million loss. National City

Bank's stock dropped more than $469 from its 1929 high to its 1933 low ($580 − 16 = $564).

The 18,300 shares "sold" to his wife by Mitchell were pledged with J. P. Morgan & Co. as collateral for a loan of $6 million (at times the loan exceeded $10 million) to finance the stock purchases. In addition, Mitchell had mortgaged his three homes to help pay for the stock purchased in 1929.

As evidence that there had been a sale, the defense revealed that:

1. Mitchell and his wife both wrote letters indicating a sale and purchase.
2. The internal revenue agent was shown the letters and knew the nature of the transaction. The agent approved Mitchell's tax return.
3. A tax lawyer advised Mitchell that the transaction was valid.

As evidence that there was not a sale the prosecution revealed that:

1. The letters did not have on them a stamp indicating a transaction had taken place.
2. The wife (Elizabeth Rend Mitchell) did not pay any cash for the stock, though she had considerable wealth.
3. Mitchell sold the stock to his wife for $212 and bought the shares back at $212 when the stock had dropped to $42½ in 1932.
4. J. P. Morgan & Co. was not told of the sales (May 18, p. 1) even though the stock was collateral for Mitchell's loan.

Obviously, there was sufficient reason for the government to reject the tax loss deduction. However, given the fact that the nature of the transaction was known and approved by the internal revenue agent, there was no valid reason to bring criminal proceedings against Mitchell.

One interesting (p. 1) headline (May 24, 1933) was "Mitchell's

Wife Missed Big Profit." She could have made $800,000 by selling in 1930. On February 14, 1930, the stock was selling at $256. Thus she could have made $44 profit per share if she sold. All she had to do was sell at the stock's post 1929 high! This revelation to the *Times* came from U.S. Attorney Thomas E. Dewey. She actually sold to her husband on March 24, 1932, when the price was $42½.

On December 26, 1930, Mitchell sold 8,500 shares of Anaconda stock to W. D. Thornton at a price of $27 and bought them back on May 4, 1931, at a price of $26⅞. The Senate inquiry questioned whether or not it was a real sale. Since this was not a part of a Mitchell tax trial we assume it was sufficiently valid to satisfy the law, if not completely beyond reproach. Obviously, this transaction had nothing to do with the 1929 crash, except that the crash created the potential for a tax loss in 1930.

The May 31, 1933, *Times* (p. 15) had an article on Secretary of Treasury Mellon's attempt to make it impossible to deduct capital losses from income. The article referred to the tax situation of the Morgan partners (they paid no taxes in 1931 and 1932 because of large capital losses). It could also have referred to Mitchell's 1929 and 1930 tax manipulations.

Mitchell was not a saint, and he wanted out of his financial difficulties. He appealed to the bank's board to pay for his loss on the bank stock. He was not specific as to what he wanted and the board did not act (*Times*, May 25, 1933, p. 1). The next day Representative Hamilton Fish (New York) was quoted as saying that the "big bankers" acted badly "inducing people to draw out funds and invest in worthless bonds." He was referring to Mitchell and Wiggin and bonds their banks had underwritten.

Mitchell's lawyer made clear that Mitchell's 1929 tax return had been approved by the Internal Revenue Service and that "the agent looked at copies of the 'Dear Charles' and 'Dear Elizabeth' letters defining the stock sale and asked for the originals" (June 1, 1933, p. 1).

Was the $666,666 income? While the $666,666 had originally been intended as income, "the company had formally notified Mr. Mitchell that the payment had been rescinded and that the amount was to be repaid later" (June 1, p. 11). Later it was established that the amount was to be paid out of his future earnings, and Mitchell did not have to repay it out of his depleted assets.

The 18,300 shares of National City Bank stock had been bought October 29, 1929 (June 6, 1933, p. 18). Mitchell said he considered selling in the market, but he did not because the market was thin and the sale would "accentuate decline." He consulted with Harry Forbes, a tax lawyer who indicated the sale to his wife was proper. Forbes testified that he did give the advice (June 9, 1933, p. 12) as long as the sale was "unconditional and in good faith." It could be that Mitchell did not sell in the market since the stock was held as collateral by J. P. Morgan & Co.

The U.S. district attorney, Medalie, attributed "a selfish motive" for the buying of the stock rather than an "altruistic" motive (June 7, 1933, p. 1).

Mitchell justified the exclusion of the $666,666 as taxable income since another bank officer, Stanley A. Russell, had an exclusion of $170,000 created by the same transaction approved by the Internal Revenue Service, thus Mitchell concluded that he could do the same as Russell.

In closing testimony Steuer said "Mitchell [I]s Victim" (June 20, 1933, p. 8), and Medalie described Mitchell's position as "Sanctimonious Rubbish" (June 21, 1933, p. 11).

On June 4 the jury debated ten hours without reaching a verdict. Mitchell, if found guilty, faced a ten-year prison term (June 22, 1933, p. 1). On June 23, 1933, page one, the headline was "Mitchell Cleared, Weeps at Verdict; Ovation in Court." The verdict was reached after the jury was out for twenty-five hours. Most of the observers (including the *Times* reporter) expected a conviction. The judge had told the jury that the $666,666 was not income if it had to be paid or if it was to be paid out of future incomes, and Mitchell thought he had to pay it.

The next day Mitchell left for a long rest. The trial had lasted almost six weeks. The prosecution had taken three weeks, the defense two, and three days were spent selecting the jury. Mitchell lost twenty-five pounds during the trial (thus some good came of the process).

The June 26, 1933, *Times* (p. 13) had a report of a talk given by Rev. C. Everett Wagner: "Wealthy Evaders of Taxes Scored." The Reverand was not pleased with the not guilty verdict.

Immediately after the acquittal the federal government sued for delinquent taxes. It wanted the tax loss from the "sale" to Mitchell's wife rejected, the $666,666 included as income, the interest on the taxes that should have been paid and a penalty for failure to pay. The tax court (Board of Tax Appeals) decided that Mitchell should pay $1,384,223. This included a penalty of $364,354 plus interest. A tax lien of $1,384,223 was filed by the government (June 29, 1936, p. 3). The Second Circuit Court of Appeals (May 11, 1937, p. 3) decided that Mitchell should pay the tax that would have been paid without the tax loss from the sale, but not the penalty (because of the previous criminal acquittal).

The tax court and the circuit court agreed the stock sale was "not genuine" (May 11, 1937, p. 3). There was no immediate payment by the purchaser (his wife). The circuit court decided the $666,666 was income since the amount could be paid "from amounts that should become due to them in the future." The recipients were not obliged to pay, and they never attempted to do so. However, the penalty did not have to be paid, since Mitchell had been acquitted of criminal charges by the jury.

The tax case went to the Supreme Court. Mitchell's counsel told the Supreme Court (January 15, 1938, p. 4) that "he gave up 30 million in '29 to 'stem [the] tide'." The government called him a "tax evader" and wanted compensation for investigating fraud. The Supreme Court awarded the compensation. In October 1937 the Supreme Court decided that Mitchell had to pay the $728,709 and on March 8, 1938, it decided that the 50 percent fine of $364,354 that had been disallowed by the Second Circuit Court of Appeals had to be paid. The penalty verdict was handed down by Judge Louis Brandeis (there was one dissent). The Court decided there was no double jeopardy (March 8, 1938, p. 2), and the outcome of the criminal case did not determine the tax to be paid.

On December 28, 1938, Mitchell settled his income tax bill for 1929. The government evaluated his assets, and the "$1,384,222 lien was settled for undisclosed sum." A government official said that the deal was "a compromise that gave Mr. Mitchell a good break."

There were many faults with the process followed by the government. Most people will conclude that Mitchell should have been asked to pay the tax, assuming the "sale" to his wife did not actually take place. The $666,666 of income (or loan) was a judgment call, but its omission was not a criminal offense, given that there was precedent for excluding it. Mitchell should not have been forced from his position as chairman of National City Bank because of these tax payment disagreements. Finally, the government should not have settled for less than the amount that the Supreme Court decided was the appropriate amount. While Mitchell's assets may not have been sufficient to pay the tax lien, his prospective incomes would be sufficient. In 1935 Mitchell was appointed chairman of the investment banking firm of Blyth & Co. and was earning enough income so that he would obviously be able to pay his tax debts, if given sufficient time.

To his credit, despite the severity of his financial difficulties, Mitchell refused to go into bankruptcy. He ultimately paid off his loans to J. P. Morgan & Co. (they did not press him during his period of difficulties). It can also be said that he paid his taxes (we do not know the amount). My preference would have been that he pay all except the penalty (the jury said he was not guilty of fraud).

It is clear that Mitchell did not have a strategy for manipulating his bank's stock. It is also clear that he thought the stock was a good buy in October 1929 (he bought). In October 1929 he made statements for the press that the market was not too high. He believed what he said.

Mitchell obviously was close to going over the line with his tax manipulations, but he deserved praise for his handling of his investments in 1929 from an ethics viewpoint. His investment strategy was flawed from a theoretical viewpoint (not enough diversification and bad timing), but there is not a hint of manipulation or self-serving trading.

In December 1939 (December 15, 1939, p. 39) Mitchell testified as an expert witness on the investment banking industry before the Temporary National Economic Committee of Congress. He denied that there was an investment banking monopoly in 1929, but admitted that if the National City Bank had not been forced to divest itself of its investment banking unit, it would have achieved a monopoly position. Thus he implicitly supported the Banking Act of 1933.

C. C. Mitchell received a bachelor of arts degree from Amherst in 1899. On graduation he went to work as a clerk for Western Electric for $10 per week. He then studied banking and became a vice president of National City Bank in 1916 and chairman of the board in 1929. In 1931, testifying before the Senate Finance Committee, Mitchell warned about dire consequences in Germany unless the debt payment schedule resulting from the World War was drastically revised. In 1932 Mitchell talked to New York City's Board of Estimate. The *New York Times* (October 23, 1932, VIII, p. 2) carried a glowing article on Mitchell's attempt to instill fiscal responsibility in the board. With reference to Mitchell it stated, "He had the reputation of being one of the frankest straight-from-the-shoulder talkers of all the financial executives whose opinions are worth quoting." This was a very respected person. He resigned (under pressure) from the National City Bank in 1933, five days after testifying before the Senate committee. In 1935 he was elected chairman of Blyth & Co. after a year as an independent financial consultant. He died on December 17, 1955, at the age of seventy-eight. The *New York Times* obituary included the statement, he "defrauded the Government of $850,000 in income taxes." A jury said he did not.

His testimony was a "factor in the passage of the Banking Act of 1933, which prohibited banks from continuing in the business of underwriting new security issues" (*Times*, December 18, 1955, p. 37). It is not obvious that his testimony should have affected the passage of this act. In 1933 there were at least nineteen *New York*

Times first-page articles dealing with Mitchell. The attention received by Mitchell should have been motivated by a real revelation as to the causes of the 1929 boom and crash, but it was not. Mitchell's criminal trial was a sad example of excessive prosecutive zeal on the part of an agency of the federal government.

ALBERT H. WIGGIN

Albert H. Wiggin was the president of Chase National Bank in 1929. He did three very strange things in 1929 or before. First, a subsidiary of Chase (Metpotan Securities Corporation) engaged in frantic trading activities that made little profit from 1928 to 1932. The total profit was less than $160,000, not including the opportunity cost on the capital used. Second, three corporations owned by Wiggin or his family engaged in longer term investing in Chase stock and made a gain of over $10 million. Third, between September 23 and November 4, 1929, Wiggin sold short 42,506 shares of Chase stock. Galbraith, Pecora, Malkiel, and the 1933 *New York Times* all cite the selling short of his own bank stock as an outrageous action. I disagree.

Between September 23 and November 4, 1929, Wiggin sold short 42,506 shares of Chase stock and made a profit of $4 million. Selling short the stock of the company of which you are president is obviously in bad taste (at a minimum). However, the facts are more involved. During the period of short sale Wiggin was long many more shares than were sold. He was "selling against the box." At the same time that he made a profit of $4 million from selling short he had much larger losses from the shares he owned.

In 1932 Chase cut its dividend from $4 to $2.25 per share, and the stock dropped to below $20. In January 1933 Wiggin, who was to be sixty-five on February 21, retired from Chase. The January 9, 1933, *Times* (p. 5) had a heading "Retiring Chase Head Sees Credit Restoration and Recovery Nearing." His views were sought and respected. On October 18, 1933, the *Times* (p. 5) reported that "Wiggin Heads Banker Club." Even retired, he was elected club president by his peers. But then the *Times* reported Wiggin's testimony before the Senate subcommittee. On page one (October 18, 1933) was the headline "Chase Bank Voted Salary of $100,000 to Wiggin for Life. Received $1,500,000 in 4½ Years Before Retirement." This was a period when $2,000 a year was a very large income.

Pecora pointed out that "loans to some of the 59 companies from which Mr. Wiggin drew salaries figured in the losses of the Chase National Bank" (October 18, 1933, p. 1). Wiggin had been a director of these fifty-nine companies in one or more of the two years studied. Pecora also focused on the bonuses received by Wiggin in compensation for the large incomes earned by his bank. Senator Adams asked if it worked the other way. Wiggin responded it "worked only one way" (October 18, 1933, p. 4).

Wiggin was born on February 21, 1868, in Medfield, Massachusetts, and began as a bank clerk in Boston immediately after graduating from high school at age seventeen. He was the son of a Unitarian clergyman. In 1904 at the age of thirty-six he became a vice president of Chase; in 1911 he became the president; and in 1918, chairman of the board. In 1904 Chase had $2 million of stock equity and $54 million of deposits. By 1930 Chase's equity was $296 million and deposits were $2 billion. It became the largest bank in the world (*Times*, October 18, 1933, p. 4). In 1931 Wiggin was chairman of the Foreign Credits Standstill Committee with the objective of preventing the collapse of Germany's financial structure. As of December 31, 1931, the Wiggin family owned 217,666 shares of Chase stock (*Times*, October 28, p. 18). In October 1933 he was called to testify before the Senate subcommittee to justify his stock transactions.

On October 19, 1933, the *Times* (p. 1) reported the financial affairs of Chase Securities Corporation. From 1917 to 1933 the Chase subsidiary had earned $41,081,956. But in 1933 after the corporation recognized a $119,000,000 write-down of assets, its sixteen-year record was a loss of $77.9 million. This highlights the inability of Wall Street insiders to take advantage of their position. Wiggin was asked his opinion of the subsidiary's performance. He responded "I think that is a very unfortunate record."

A page one headline (October 20, 1933) blared "Wiggin Pool

Sold Chase Bank Stock." The pool was in April 1928 and it bought $113,240,356 of Chase Bank stock (the pool could not hold more than 1,800 shares at one time) and sold this stock for $113,290,977, a gain of $50,620 (not counting the opportunity cost on the capital). The stock price had gone up from $580 to $687 during the life of the pool, but the gain was close to zero. Wiggin indicated that the purposes of the pool were to keep a steady market in the stock, achieve a wider market and, for some of the pool members, to make money (October 20, 1933, p. 8). There were other syndicates to follow. They tended to make very modest gains. It is difficult to see what the syndicates achieved and why they focused on Chase's stock. Wiggin's explanations do not satisfy.

Thomas Lamont (J. P. Morgan & Co.), in a 1929 telegram to Wiggin, invited him to buy ten thousand shares of Alleghany Corporation at $20 when the market was $35 (October 21, 1933, p. 21). Senator Couzens asked, "Did you make any money out of it?" Wiggin responded, "No. I lost money." Pecora then asked, "That is because you did not take advantage of the market at the time?" Pecora wanted Wiggin to sell at the stock's high (speculate?) rather than hold (invest?). Very strange.

On October 25, 1933 (p. 33), there was an article with the heading "Protests Wiggin Pension." The controller of the City of Baltimore, a shareholder of Chase, protested that Wiggin would receive $100,000 for life while no employee (including the mayor) of the City of Baltimore received as much as $10,000 per year. On October 26 the *Times* (p. 1) reported "Wiggin Gives Up $100,000 a Year Under Criticism." His offer was accepted by the board.

On October 28, 1933 (p. 1), the new Chase chairman, Winthrop W. Aldrich, made the headline: "Aldrich Disavows Bank Pool Policies of Wiggin Regime." Aldrich indicated that the bank would not engage in such activities during his time as chairman.

On the same day Pecora said that Wiggin "had realized profits of $10,425,657.02 in open market transactions of the Chase National Bank in the five-year period 1928–32." These were cash profits reported as income in the tax returns. On October 29, 1933 (p. 27), there was an expansion of this gain: "$10,000,000 was small share of the total gains to the banker from trading in securities."

Chase stock reached a high of $285 in 1929 and a low of $135. It dropped to below $20 in 1933. At the end of 1932, the Wiggin family owned 194,000 shares. Wiggin estimated that the family corporations had lost $5,139,097.90 based on market values (November 1, 1933, p. 17).

Wiggin was asked why he used family corporations. He explained that the 12½ percent corporate tax rate was less than that paid by individuals (24 percent in 1929). The article (November 1, 1933, p. 17) concluded with the statement that the Internal Revenue Service was reviewing Wiggin's tax returns.

The November 2, 1933, *Times* (p. 1) had the headline "Tax Saving Deals Related by Wiggin: He Paid $4,624,905." The taxes paid were for the years 1928–1932. The *Times* admitted, "The size of the Wiggin family tax payments came as a surprise." In a sense Wiggin had to prove his innocence.

There is no court case involving Wiggin. The government looked hard but could not find the basis of even a bad set of accusations. The short sale was his major "crime." But consider the fact that as of October 9, 1929, the Wiggin family owned 116,528 shares. He sold short 42,506 shares, thus he still had a net investment of 74,022 shares. Using the 1929 low price of $135 this is a net investment of $9,992,970. Using the high prices of the dates of short sale the Chase stock price went down by approximately $100 so Wiggin made $4,250,000 by selling short. But during the same period he lost $11,652,800 in market value. Thus he lost a net $7,402,200 on the Chase investment (an unrealized loss) from September to December 1929.

Wiggin started selling short on September 23, 1929. This, of course, was pure genius, unless he had inside information. Since the drop in value of the Chase stock was caused by the market crash, not firm specific information, it would be unfair to accuse Wiggin of insider trading.

Why did Wiggin not sell 42,506 shares that he owned, rather than selling short that number of shares? It is obvious that Wiggin was sensitive to taxes. He had large unrealized tax gains, and could not sell any of his shares without incurring a large tax bill. Thus, the sensible thing to do from a tax strategy viewpoint was to sell Chase stock short, if he wanted to reduce his exposure to risk. By selling short he avoided the capital gains tax that he would have to pay by selling the stock he held. The motivation was to save taxes, not to exploit insider information. He only sold short an amount of stock equal to a fraction of the shares he owned.

On September 5, 1929, the *Times* (p. 46) reported that Chase National Bank had declared a quarterly dividend of $1 per share. The *Times* on September 10 (p. 36) expanded on the dividend story. The $4 per share annual rate was a $.40 per share increase over the previous annual rate of $3.60 (it had been $18 per share but there was then a five-to-one stock split). These are the only two news releases regarding Chase that were made during the last four months of 1929. There was no obvious news regarding Chase that would lead to a sell decision in September or October 1929 based on insider information. Wiggin waited until well after the good news of the dividend increase before selling the 42,506 shares short.

On January 7, 1930 (p. 40) there was an article in the *Times* acclaiming the virtues of Chase: "Chase Bank Assets Now $1,714,829,447"; "New High Record for Deposits Also Reported." This was followed on January 15 (p. 40) with an article revealing Chase's profits for 1929 of $24,080,254 (the dividend was $15,990,000). In 1929, Chase was the second largest bank (based on capital) in the United States. On March 20, 1930 (p. 38), the intended merger of Chase, Equitable Trust Company, and Interstate Trust Company was described. This merger would make Chase the largest bank in the world. On June 2 the merger was completed and bank stocks went up. On July 7, 1930, the *Times* (p. 1) headlined "Chase Bank Funds Set World Record."

Wiggin sold short from September 23 to November 4, 1929, when there was no specific news applicable to Chase. In December he covered his short position. Given the reports of good news concerning Chase that were to appear in the first seven months of 1930, the covering of the short position was just in time. It could be that

Wiggin covered his short position based on insider information. The sequence of events reveals why it was ill-advised for Wiggin to first sell and then buy Chase stock in 1929, if he wanted to appear ethical. It is possible that at least one of the sell or buy transactions was motivated by information not available to a public investor.

There is an interesting ethical question. If a manager owns a large number of shares in his company, can the manager ethically sell some or all of those shares if he wants liquidity (cash), diversification, or is of the opinion that the market is too high and is likely to fall? Of course, now the manager can short the market index. In 1929 the practice of sophisticated investors with a large capital gain was to "sell against the box." This is what Wiggin did.

An editorial (*Times*, November 2, p. 20) that was headed "An Enemy Hath Not Done This" indicated that banking had "much reason to dread what is done by some of its friends." Speaking of Wiggin the editor criticizes "the irregularity and impropriety of his enormous dealings in the stock of his own bank, going so far as to sell it 'short' just before the financial crash in 1929." The editor should at least mention Wiggin's large net investment in his bank's stock, after selling short!

The editorial goes on to say that the testimony was a "great shock to public confidence in our banking system." The editor could have added "and confidence in the ability of our newspapers to be objective."

A letter to the editor (November 10, p. 20) verifies that the editorials and news articles had found their mark: "Doubtless the panic of 1929 was due largely to many in control of large interests, financial and industrial" (H. L. Young). Chase National Bank stock hit a high of $283 in 1929 and then declined to $17.75 in 1933. Assuming the Wiggin family owned 116,528 shares (their actual holding as of October 9, 1929) this would be a loss of $30,909,052. Their actual holdings as of December 31, 1931, were 217,666, so the $30,909,052 estimated loss was not unreasonable. Wiggin estimated a price decline from 1929 to 1932 of $240 per share and the family holdings at the end of 1932 of 194,000 shares. This leads to a loss of $46,560,000 (Pecora, 1933, pp. 2851–52). Again we have a situation in which a Wall Street insider suffered a major loss just as did the average American shareholder. It is unfair to suggest that Wiggin caused the selling panic or that he profited greatly from the market decline.

Pecora wanted Wiggin to define "speculation." He asked Wiggin, "Now, speculative operations very often are successful, too, aren't they, and result in a profit to the speculator?" Wiggin responded "I think they used to be." There was laughter (Pecora, 1933, p. 2419).

In the summer of 1932 there were stock transactions involving Wiggin and Brooklyn Manhattan Transit Company (BMT) that were not ethical in 1932 and would be illegal today. Newspapers reported that Wiggin's Shermar Corporation, Chase, and Gerhard M. Dahl, chairman of BMT's board of directors, sold BMT stock in June 1932 immediately before the company "passed" a dividend on its common stock. Wiggin was chairman of the company's finance committee and "was convinced that the company, because of its then financial difficulties, ought to pass a dividend on its common stock" (*Times*, November 3, 1933, p. 1). Wiggin was paid $20,000 a year for his efforts as chairman of the finance committee.

In the second quarter of 1932, the dividend was passed. The stock went from a price of $25 on June 4 to a price of $11 on June 8. Even the implementation of the sale was somewhat suspect (Shermar Corporation first sold 8,700 shares and the next day Chase sold). Dahl was heavily in debt to Chase, and Chase held his BMT stock as collateral. In June 1932 Wiggin's corporation (Shermar) owned 26,400 shares of BMT. The June transactions were (*Times*, November 3, 1933, p. 12):

June 3, 1932	Shermar sold 8,700 shares
June 4, 1932	Chase National sold 50,000 shares pledged by Dahl and held by Chase as collateral
June 6, 1932	Shermar sold 17,700 shares
	Chase sold 5,000 shares

Even before insider trading became illegal there was a type of justice. The BMT stock in 1933 closed at $27 during the day that Wiggin testified. He lost by selling in 1932 (unless he bought the stock back at $11), but it was still wrong of him to sell.

Senator Fletcher (*Times*, November 4, 1933, p. 12) immediately declared the need for legislation to prevent trading based on insider information.

There was immediately a move to "drop Dahl and Wiggin" from the management of BMT. On November 6, 1933 (p. 27), there was an article explaining that Dahl protested the stock sale. Dahl said the stock was "sold by Mr. Wiggin, as then head of the Chase Bank over my protest and over my objection." A letter by Wiggin written at the time of the sale acknowledged Dahl's objection. Thus Dahl was innocent of the insider trading charge. Wiggin only was responsible for selling the stock. Wiggin deserved censure for these transactions.

On May 22, 1951, Albert Wiggin died at an age of eighty-three. He left an estate of $18,975,204 including 47,599 shares of Chase stock (*Times*, February 5, 1955, p. 16). He left his collection of art books to the Boston Library.

Up until the time of the hearings, Albert H. Wiggin was the classic Horatio Alger success story. The 1933 hearings revealed the mistake of Chase subsidiaries trading excessively in Chase stock achieving no apparent purpose, certainly not profit. But the hearings revealed no crimes (the BMT sale was unethical but it was not a crime in 1932), and equally important they revealed nothing to indicate that either the actions of Wiggin or Chase caused the October 1929 crash. Pecora states, "In the entire investigation, it is doubtful if there was another instance of a corporate executive who so thoroughly and successfully used his official and fiduciary position for private profit" (Pecora, 1939, p. 161). Wiggin did several things that he should not have done with Chase stock, but the trading activities were ineffective and only the short sale of Chase stock appeared to be dramatically incorrect. But even after the short sale he was left with a net long position of over seventy thousand shares of Chase stock immediately before the market crashed. The sale by Wiggin of BMT stock in 1932 based on insider information was an unethical act, but obviously it did not affect the 1929 crash.

SAM INSULL

Samuel Insull built a massive, complicated public utility holding company empire. After the crash of 1929–1932, Insull was charged with using the mails to defraud, violating the Bankruptcy Act, and embezzlement. He was tried and acquitted of all charges in three different trials.

Essentially Insull was hounded and then charged with crimes because his firm went bankrupt and investors lost money. But the reasons the investors lost were the downturn in the market, the fact that Insull's firms were highly levered, and the development of a worldwide depression. These are not crimes of Insull.

Sam Insull was born in England on November 11, 1859. At age fourteen he stopped going to school and began work as an apprentice clerk at five shillings ($1.25) a week. At the height of his career he controlled over $3 billion of assets and had personal wealth of between $75 and $300 million. After his fall he was left with an income of $21,000 a year (a large sum in 1932).

The *New York Times* obituary (July 17, 1938, p. 26) included the nasty comment "There is no record of personal philanthropy... except for a $100,000 gift to London Temperance Hospital." His parents, Samuel and Emma, favored temperance. The comment regarding his gift giving was unfair. In one of his trials the prosecution used his tax returns to show how outrageously large were his earnings. But "Insull's charitable contributions were also enormous, amounting in several years to more than his entire income from salaries" (McDonald, 1962, p. 331). Also the October 24, 1930, *New York Times* (p. 2) announced that "Insull Forces Give Part of Pay to Idle." The workers in Insull's empire, on a voluntary basis, were each to give one day's pay per month to the unemployed.

Insull's first job ended when he "got the sack." He hit his boss's son when that unfortunate accused him of stealing stamps. After several short term employments he worked for Colonel E. H. Johnson, the manager of Thomas A. Edison's London operations. In 1881 when Insull was twenty-one he arrived in New York and with the help of an introduction from Johnson, immediately sought out Thomas A. Edison. Insull knew shorthand and bookkeeping and went to work as Edison's secretary. He soon became more than the average secretary. He helped Edison organize the Electric Tube Company and then in 1889 the Edison General Electric Company (yes, this was *the* General Electric Company). Insull became the vice president in charge of manufacturing and selling.

When the opportunity to be the manager of Chicago Edison Company became available, he asked for and got that position at one-third the salary he was offered to stay at General Electric as president. This launched his career in public utilities.

He believed the securities of a utility serving a city should be owned by the people it served. By 1907 Chicago Edison had evolved into Chicago Commonwealth Edison and it had an electric utility monopoly in Chicago. By 1912 the utility holding company Middle West Utilities serviced 1,718,000 customers, had 600,000 security holders, 324 steam plants, and 196 hydro-electric plants.

Insull had a readily charming smile as well as a fiery temper. He was quick to take offense. His management style is interesting (*Times*, July 17, 1938, p. 26). "He roared a little louder than the others; thumped his desk; made snap decisions, overriding the more cautious." This style led to a series of significant operating innovations that changed the industry. He innovated with turbines, transmission lines, and location and size of plants. He was an important person in the economic development of the United States during the nineteen twenties.

His list of honors is long. For example:

He lectured at Princeton (1921).

He received honorary degrees at

    Union College (1917),

    Northwestern (1926),

    Notre Dame (1926), and

    Queen's University (1930).

He was made a Knight of Legion of Honor (France).

He received the Charles A. Coffin Medal of the National Electric Light Association (1926).

In 1929 he headed the syndicate that completed the task of raising $20 million to build a new forty-six-story Chicago Civic Opera House. In 1931 Martin Insull, Sam's brother, was made a trustee of Cornell University. Then came the crash, the economic slowdown, and the collapse of Insull's empire.

On June 6, 1932, Insull resigned as chairman or president of eighty-five companies. His brother (Martin) and he had spent their fortunes trying to prevent the bankruptcy of his holding company; thus when bankruptcy arrived, Sam Insull was the biggest financial loser of all the investors in his empire. This fact was ignored when the federal government tried to punish the person they thought was one of those who caused the 1929 crash and the 1932 depression.

Garfield Charles, special referee in bankruptcy, wrote a report (*Times*, March 27, 1938, p. 25) in which he stated that the $56 million Insull paid Cyrus Eaton for securities in the Insull companies was excessive and was the primary cause of the Insull failure. In the current language of finance, Insull was paying greenmail to Eaton. Eaton was challenging Insull's control, so Insull, given the opportunity, bought him out in 1930. Insull did not own enough shares to guarantee control of his corporations; thus Eaton's threat to his control was real. Unfortunately, the timing of the purchase from Eaton was very bad and the amount paid was too large. The $48 million of short-term debt used by Insull to finance the purchase was certainly a factor in the collapse of the Insull empire.

Owen D. Young, in reviewing the collapse and the complexity of the Insull organization, said that Insull must have found it incomprehensible and asked "how could the public which purchased the securities be expected to comprehend it" (*Times*, February 17, 1933, p. 1). Consider the following arrangement. Corporate Securities (controlled by Insull) issued 1,250,000 shares of stock to Corporate Syndicates Inc. (owned by Corporate Securities) and Insull, Son &

Co. (a subsidiary of Insull Utility Investment, Inc.). The above securities were sold at a gain to Utilities Securities Co. The consolidation of the financial statements must have been an intellectual challenge.

Knowing that there were investigations into his affairs, on June 22, 1932, Insull went to Paris and from there went to Athens, Greece. The United States demanded that he be extradited. He was arrested in Greece on October 10 and was released (inadequate grounds for extradition). He was arrested again on November 4 and was again released.

The United States voided his passport in 1933, and in addition, his $21,000-a-year pension was cut off. The Greek government told him he had to leave by January 1, 1934, and then revised the date to March 15, 1934. There followed several escapes by freighter and travel to Turkey. When he was taken off a Greek ship in Turkish waters by Turkey there was a major international incident. He landed in the United States on May 7, 1934. His refusal to return voluntarily for trial was taken by many to be an admission of guilt. He claimed he fled because he could not get a fair trial given the political climate. A reading of the newspapers, and one would then associate the name Insull with financial crime.

Upon his arrival in the United States, his bail was set at $200,000. He stayed in jail since he had used his wealth in his failed, but ethical, efforts to save his companies. Finally, bail for the seventy-four-year-old man was reduced to $10,000, and he was released on bail.

In 1933 the *Times* reported that Senator Norbeck, chairman of the subcommittee investigating the stock exchange, stated (February 7, p. 3), "We have been working a long time investigating the Insull connection with the Stock Exchange." But Insull's personal financial connection began in 1930, not 1929.

The first trial was in federal court and the charge was using the mail to defraud. Insull, his son, and colleagues were all acquitted. The second trial was for embezzlement in a state court. Insull was acquitted. The third trial was for violation of the bankruptcy act in federal court, and Judge John C. Know "directed a verdict of acquittal" (*Times*, July 17, 1938, p. 26).

In February 1936, Insull helped start the "Affiliated Broadcasting Company," but he lost control and gave up his position with the company.

On July 17, 1938, the *Times* headline was "Insull Drops Dead in a Paris Subway—20 Cents in His Pocket." He was seventy-eight years old and alone when he died. His wife was with him at a Paris hotel but she was shopping. Her comment on learning of his death was "Poor man, he has suffered so much in the last 20 years!"

The *Times* of 1937 and 1938 contained article after article (each very short) dealing with the aftermath of the collapse of Insull's empire. Many dealt with the conflict between the banks and the holders of notes and debentures as they fought over the remains. But the really sad stories were the sale of the personal possessions of Samuel and his wife Margaret. For example, a manuscript of Lafcadio Hearn sold for less than $1,000 and a signed manuscript of Joyce Kilmer's "Trees" sold for $620 (*Times*, February 19, 1937, p. 17). On June 27, 1937, the entire furnishings of Insull's home, valued at $100,000, were sold for $26,000 (*Times*, June 27, 1937, p. 6).

On September 23, 1953, Mrs. Sam Insull (age eighty) died. After the loss of the family wealth she had stated, "You know, I don't even miss the money. I suppose I had too much" (*New York Times*, September 24, 1953, p. 33). Margaret A. Bird (Mrs. Sam Insull) had a stage name of Gladys Wallis.

Insull did not cause the 1929 crash, but his operating companies and his holding companies did use a large amount of leverage. Add the leverage of the investment trusts and the leverage of investors, and we have investments that were very sensitive to the level of utility company stock prices. The problem was not Insull's criminal acts (which the courts concluded did not exist) but rather his failure to appreciate fully the riskiness of the capital structures that he and others were using. Once stock prices started to tumble the buyers of utility stocks were in trouble. Once economic activity started to slacken (1929–1932) then Insull's financial empire was destroyed. The same analysis applies to more than sixty other public utility holding companies existing in the period 1929–1933.

CONCLUSIONS

The inquiry into the affairs of J. P. Morgan in May 1933 by the U.S. Senate received a large number of large front page (*Times*) headlines. One of the more significant was (May 30) "Roosevelt Backs Morgan Inquiry." Despite the President's backing the inquiries revealed nothing significant. The former vice governor of the Federal Reserve Board and then vice president of Marine Midland Corporation of New York, Edmund Platt, was reported on July 4 (p. 22) as saying that the Senate investigation was "in charge of a clever prosecuting attorney from New York who knows nothing of economics and whose purpose appeared to be to discredit all bankers and to make things appear wrong that are not wrong." Platt's statement was on page twenty-two. The reports of Pecora's questioning of Morgan and Mitchell were repeatedly on page one. Platt declared that the treatment of J. P. Morgan "was a disgrace to the Senate." He then listed the financial and economic information that would have been useful (international transactions, flow of gold, money markets, etc.).

A *Times* article by Arthur Krock (May 31, p. 16), referring to President Roosevelt's approval of the Senate inquiry, said that Congress "will not deny the people victims when victims are demanded. The bankers must taste the sands of the arena."

Schwed (1940, p. 196) said it well. "The crookedness of Wall Street is in my opinion an overrated phenomenon . . . they suggest to the public an excuse for the public's own folly."

There were acts in 1929 and the years following that would not pass a reasonable ethics test. But it is not logical to blame these acts for the 1929 crash. Also, most of the mistakes were "honest mistakes." The real crime was the persecution by the federal government of business people who had made wrong decisions but were not criminals.

CHAPTER 9

An Overview of the Causes
of the Crash

The market reached a peak on September 19, 1929, and then started to slide. But the crash actually picked up momentum on October 3. On that day the news report of the talk by Philip Snowden, the British chancellor of the exchequer, concerning the "orgy of American speculation" was reported by the newspapers. The Hatry collapse was old news by October 3, but the consequences to British investors were still relevant.

On August 8 the Federal Reserve Bank of New York increased the rediscount rate from 5 to 6 percent. This increase was approved by the Federal Reserve Board and was the strongest action taken by the board since its letter of February 2, 1929, to all Federal Reserve Banks. The February 2 letter stated, "A member bank is not within its reasonable claims for rediscount facilities at its Federal Reserve Bank when it borrows either for the purpose of making speculative loans or for the purpose of maintaining speculative loans" (Bierman, 1991, p. 100). Both of these actions were reinforced by repeated messages from the members of the Federal Reserve Board for banks not to make loans to support speculative investments, reducing the inclination of the New York banks to finance broker loans.

In September stock prices peaked and started a slight slide. The action of the New York Federal Reserve Bank to increase the discount rate from 5 to 6 percent on August 8 was not a significant factor in September. On September 26 the Bank of England raised its discount rate from 5½ to 6½ percent. This event was significant. The 6½ percent rate was higher than the dividend yield on stocks, the yield of investment grade bonds, and during October was higher than the return on call money being used by the stock market. Some English investors shifted funds from New York to London.

J. Maynard Keynes (*Listener*, October 2, 1921, p. 435) offered explanations why the interest rate was raised by the Bank of England from 5½ to 6½ percent. The primary explanation was that £40 million of gold had flowed out of the Bank of England in the preceding twelve months. This was 25 percent of England's stock of gold. England was losing gold because of the stock market investments in America by the English despite a favorable balance of trade of between £100 and £150 million.

Keynes conjectured that the results of the interest rate increase would be a decrease in foreign borrowing, less investment domestically, and higher unemployment. He concluded that the first result was the only one sought, "that investors will be reluctant for the present, to subscribe to new loans to overseas." Interestingly, he did not conjecture (in print) at all as to the effect the rate increase would have on New York Stock Exchange stock prices.

On October 12 new call money yielded 5.63 percent invested in New York (Wigmore, 1985, p. 627). This rate reflected an abundance of loan funds to finance securities in October. British investors were nervous, given the Hatry experience, and were also required to cover margin account losses caused by the Hatry collapse. The *New York Times* secondary headline (p. 1) of October 4 was "Year's Worst Break Hits Stock Market." This break coincided with Snowden's "orgy" statement. Utility stocks were hit hard during October 3, and there were news reports concerning Federal Trade Commission hearings in Washington regarding utility mergers.

The next significant market date is Wednesday, October 16, a decline caused by a news story reported on October 12. From October 4 to October 12 the papers carried no obvious significant news for the market. Brokers' loans were up, but only marginally. The cost of call money bounced between 5 and 6 percent, and call money was in "abundance."

On Saturday, October 12 (after the stock market had closed), there was the news report of the famous Massachusetts commission decision barring Boston Edison from a stock split. On Wednesday, October 16, the *Times* (p. 42) reported that the Massachusetts regulators were also going to review the firm's rates. New York State and the Federal Trade Commission were also conducting hearings with negative implications for investors. The Thursday, October 17, *Times* (p. 38) reported "Stocks Decline Sharply." There were also negative news articles concerning utility regulation on October 17.

The next major date was Thursday, October 24 (Black Thursday). Between October 16 and October 24, while there were no major news reports, several things were happening. The public utility inquiries continued, making the public utility segment of the market nervous (a term used frequently by the press). New stock issues of investment trusts and the increasing level of brokers' loans continued to be of interest to the newspapers. There were minor articles in the *Times* (October 21, p. 38) titled "Undigested Securities" and (p. 40) "Europe Recalling Capital From Here." The withdrawal of European capital was a contributing factor to the shaky market.

On Monday, October 21, stocks went down in the third largest trading day on record. There were heavy margin calls.

The Wednesday, October 23, *Times* (p. 38) reported Babson's recommendation to sell, and on Wednesday the stocks lost $4 billion of value, but this is not a famous day since the next day was Black Thursday. On Thursday, October 24, there occurred the "Worst Stock Crash" (October 25, p. 1). On Friday and Saturday stocks "held firm."

On Monday, October 28, stocks lost another $14 billion. Still the news articles were optimistic for the future. But the next day was Black Tuesday, October 29, and stocks collapsed in a sixteen million share day. The drop in value on this single day was 17.3 percent.

The *New York Times* (October 30, p. 1) estimated the following October losses for a sample of 115 stocks:

Industry	Number of Stocks	Decline in Value
Railroads	25	$1,129 million
Public Utilities	29	5,136 million
Motors	15	1,000 million
Oils	22	1,333 million
Coppers	15	824 million
Chemicals	9	1,622 million

These numbers do not "prove" that public utilities declined the most (percentage losses would have been more useful), but they would certainly imply to a reader of the *Times* that the utility industry had been the hardest hit.

The *Times* estimated the loss for Black Tuesday (October 29) at between $8 and $9 billion.

LOANS BY "OTHERS"

As the Federal Reserve Board made it more difficult for the banks to lend to brokers in 1928 and 1929, the loans by "others" increased. In 1927 loans by "others" were $800 million. By the end of September 1929 the amount was $3,860 million. The *Economist* (December 7, 1929, p. 1070) identified the source of a large percentage of these funds as "foreign short money." This money was very sensitive to small changes in interest rates.

On September 26, 1929, the Bank of England, reacting to a loss of gold, raised its discount rate from 5½ to 6½ percent. Only in 1907, 1914, and 1920 had the rate been higher in the twentieth century. The *New York Times* London correspondent said that the rate increase (December 31, 1929, p. 25) "produced in Lombard's Street's opinion, the first crack in Wall Street's speculative edifice." The correspondent also mentioned Hatry: "This event led many persons here, who were taking a hand in the Wall Street Gamble to withdraw."

Both the French and German *Times* correspondents indicated that there was a relatively small amount of speculation from those sources. The Paris correspondent stated (December 31, p. 25), "Not that the French took a large part in the Wall Street speculation." The message from Berlin was that "German holdings were limited."

Table 9.1
Exchange Rates Using the High Price of the Day

	English	French	German	Holland
January 5	4.84⅞	3.90¹³⁄₁₄	23.80	40.16
October 5	4.86⅛*	3.92⅝	23.84	40.16½
November 2	4.87⅝	3.94	23.93½	40.35½
December 28	4.87¹³⁄₁₆	3.94⅜	23.96	40.37

*The maximum price in October was 4.87⁷⁄₁₆ (*Economist*, February 15, 1930, p. 72).

An inspection of the exchange rates for 1929 reflects that English, French, German, and Holland investors tended to be selling dollars, as shown in Table 9.1.

The *Wall Street Journal* (November 7, 1929, p. 1) did not think that the departure of the foreign funds was the result of a master plan or that the departure was the primary cause of the crash. It stated its position clearly: "Another piece of front page claptrap was a cable from London . . . stating that the market had been broken by foreign sales of stock and withdrawals of borrowed money." The *Journal* concluded, "It is respectfully submitted that good intentions, where people are dealing with a subject they do not begin to understand, do not excuse the resulting ignorance and confusion."

A SUMMARY OF CAUSES

The media and people of influence warned of excessive speculation in the New York stock market. The Hatry collapse created uneasiness in England regarding stocks in general. On October 3 Snowden's "orgy of speculation" talk coincided with a market slide. This weakened the position of margin accounts.

Starting on October 12 there were expanded attacks on public utilities by the regulatory commissions in Massachusetts and New York. On October 16 there was a second major stock market break, further weakening margin accounts. Margin accounts were called, and European capital flowed out of New York.

On October 24, Black Thursday, and October 29, Black Tuesday, massive losses occurred with no further news motivating the selling. The losses seemed to occur because of margin selling, foreign capital leaving New York, and a general reaction to news articles saying the break was inevitable and was overdue. In addition, there is the claim of this book, that the decline in value of $5,136 million for twenty-nine public utilities reported by the *New York Times* on October 30 was the result of a clearly defined overvaluation of public utility stocks given the bad news regarding the regulatory climate. If the public utility stocks were not overvalued before the news from Massachusetts, New York, and Washington, they were overvalued after these news reports.

Highly levered investment trusts, heavily invested in overpriced public utility stocks, were a very vulnerable stock market segment. Public utility holding companies also added their leverage to the already levered utility sector. Finally, recognizing that the levered investment trusts were purchased by individual investors with 50 percent borrowed funds, we have a classic case of excessive leverage, if we consider all the levels of leverage. Thus in summary we have:

The federal government's "war" on speculators—making all investors nervous and resulting in an August increase by the Federal Reserve Board in the rediscount rate at Federal Reserve banks.

The August 8 increase by the New York Federal Reserve Bank of the rediscount rate from 5 to 6 percent.

The Hatry affair—making British investors nervous and forcing some liquidation of U.S. investments.

The Bank of England increasing the discount rate to 6½ percent on September 26, 1929, resulting in a flow of investment funds from New York to London.

Snowden's "orgy" statement—triggering the October 3, 1929, sell-off and a continuing concern.

Public utility bashing—FTC, Massachusetts, and New York

State all contributed to heightened concern. Boston Edison's bad news was first published on October 12, 1929 and was repeated throughout October.

Public utilities overpriced—the bashing was significant since the public utility stocks were overpriced, if not before the bashing, then certainly after it.

Holding companies, investment trusts, and margin buying—all added to the investors' leverage and compounded the problem of overpriced public utility stocks.

Foreign capital fleeing New York—an additional factor adding pressure on prices.

The market's overreaction—once the selling began the panic was contagious.

All of the above elements made their contribution to the October 1929 crash. Without the overpriced public utility stocks the market would have had an adjustment, but not necessarily a crash of the severity experienced. Without the depression that followed, the 36 percent loss suffered in 1929 (September to December 31) would have been hurtful, but nothing like the value loss in excess of 70 percent that was to occur from September 1929 to 1933.

A long passage of time was required before observers could look at October 1929 in an objective fashion. The investigations by the U.S. Congress in 1933–1935 and the accusations made were not objective. Fortunately, while several people were unjustly brought to criminal trial, they were found innocent. The blame for 1929 is not to be found in a few inhabitants of lower Manhattan or Chicago. The primary blame has to be shared by those investors who were too optimistic about the ability of public utilities to justify price-book value multiples in excess of three, a public utility commission eager to protect the consumers, and those public officials who sought to bring down the speculators.

AFTER THE OCTOBER CRASH

After the October crash Senator J. T. Robinson of Arkansas (the Democratic floor leader) blasted the Republican administration, especially Hoover and Mellon. Robinson accused them of having "fostered [an] era of disastrous speculation" (*New York Times*, October 31, 1929, p. 3). He was critical that they had not taken steps "to prevent the collapse, which they should have known must follow the orgy of speculation stimulated by their utterances." Snowden's "orgy" comment is again influential.

Senator A. R. Robinson, Republican of Indiana, was quick to see the inconsistency of J. T. Robinson's accusations. He stated, "Neither has suggested in any way . . . that people should gamble in the market" (*Times*, November 2, 1929, p. 2). No one worked harder than Hoover to have the stock market crash (see his memoirs). Hoover did nothing to foster an "era of disastrous speculation." He helped end the stock market prosperity.

Mellon made few public announcements. At the beginning of the year 1929 he did describe a healthy economy, and in March he recommended good bonds as an investment alternative. He never encouraged speculation.

A. R. Robinson, having logically rejected the accusations of J. T. Robinson, then made unsubstantiated accusations of his own. He blamed John J. Raskob, national chairman of the Democratic Party, for "urging the public to buy stocks" (*Times*, November 2, p. 2). Raskob was on the board of directors of many banks and industrial corporations including General Motors Corporation and E. I. DuPont de Nemours & Co. He had very publicly been in and out of the market in 1928 and 1929. In November 1929 he was instrumental in saving County Trust Co. from likely financial difficulties (its president had committed suicide). He was also involved with some of the investment pools that were popular in the late twenties. But none of this makes Raskob responsible for the 1929 stock price increases or for their collapse.

Alfred P. Sloan, the chairman of General Motors Corporation, returning from a business trip to Europe, called the events in the market a mystery and said "I cannot see any logical reason for any such action as has occurred with present market conditions." He predicted a record last quarter profit for General Motors (*Times*, November 2, 1929 p. 2).

After the crash, explanations were sought, the *Economist* (November 2, 1929, p. 825) complained that the boom was based on "future prospects" and "capitalizing the equity." The *Economist* did not want investors to consider growth prospects (p. 825) "It may well be that the traditional criterion of investment status—current profit-earning capacity—will come into its own again." This cannot be a major factor as we list causes of the crash. The use of excessively large growth rate assumptions can lead to excessively high prices. But who would currently advocate consistently leaving out growth prospects in valuing a stock? The *Economist* missed on this diagnosis.

Another explanation offered by the *Economist* (November 9, 1929, p. 867) was equally weak. This was an excessive flotation of investment trust securities. In the words of the *Economist*, these were "undigested securities." However, it also noted that public utilities had been overpriced, but aside from citing the price increases during 1929, it offered no logic for concluding that the prices were too high.

George Harrison, governor of the Federal Reserve Bank of New York in 1929, testified in the 1931 hearings of the Senate Committee on Banking and Currency held on January 1931. He was asked by the chairman (Peter Norbeck of South Dakota) why the turn in stock prices occurred. Harrison listed:

1. a business decline in July;

2. the Hatry failure;

3. an increase in the New York banks' rediscount rate in August;

4. the increase of the Bank of England rediscount rate;

5. "Things had gotten so top-heavy."

E. H. H. Simmons (*New York Times*, January 26, 1930, pp. 9 and 16), president of the New York Stock Exchange, in a talk gave five reasons for the 1929 crash:

1. high level of stock prices (low dividend yields)
2. high price earnings multipliers
3. economic disturbances abroad (Hatry, Berlin stock exchange, Austria and France)
4. overproduction in industry
5. lack of equilibrium in buying and selling

He cited the issuance of $2.3 billion of new equity securities in the first ten months of 1929. Most of these securities were issued by investment trusts and finance companies. Some of the funds were then invested in non-U.S. securities.

Simmons's list is not very convincing, but there was extensive interest in his thoughts in 1930. Simmons rejected the importance of short-selling activity. He described a survey conducted by the exchange (*New York Times*, January 26, 1930, pp. 9, 16): "The amount of the total short interest at the close of one of the worst days of the panic was found to be extraordinarily small, constituting only about one-seventh of 1 percent of the total listed shares."

There were many tongue-in-cheek explanations for the crash. For example, Senator Thomas (Democrat from Oklahoma) offered the following (*Times*, December 15, 1929, p. 2): "The stock market crash was caused by a riot break out in the Wall Street stadium in a post-season speculative game between the 'Coolidge Bulls' and young 'Hoover Bears.'"

The *New York Times Magazine* (November 2, 1930, p. 19) identified the source of the term "bear market" as being the expression "to sell the bear's skin before one has caught the bear."

CONCLUSIONS

There is no question that the fear of speculation pushed the stock market to the brink of collapse. It is entirely possible that Hoover's aggressive campaign against speculation, helped by the overpriced public utilities hit by the Massachusetts Public Utility Commission and the vulnerable margin investors, brought about the October 24 selling panic and the consequences that followed.

An important triggering event was Snowden's reference to the speculative orgy in America. The resulting decline in stock prices weakened margin positions, and when the several governmental bodies indicated that public utilities in the future were not going to be able to justify their market prices, the decreases in utility stock prices further weakened margin positions and brought on additional selling. On Black Thursday (October 24) the selling panic (an overreaction to events) started, and the 1929 stock market crash resulted.

CHAPTER 10

The 1929 Market and the 1990s

In 1929 the majority of the press and the federal government agreed that the stocks listed on the New York Stock Exchange (actually, some were on the Curb Exchange and some were unlisted) were too high. During 1929 the stocks increased in value by 35 percent from January 1 to September 19 (in 1929 dividends on common stock increased in total amount by 30 percent). In October 1929 the investors acted on the belief that stocks were too high, and the market crashed.

But compare the 1929 financial information with that of the mid 1990s. The dividend yield of stock listed on the New York stock exchange in the 1990s was consistently well below 3 percent. In 1929 it exceeded 3 percent. In November of 1996 the dividend yield of the Standard & Poor's 500 stock index fell below 2 percent.

The price-earnings ratios for the Standard & Poor's 500 stocks ranged from 16 to 25 in the 1990's. The P/E's during 1929 were well within that range, with the one exception being the high prices of September 1929. But by October, stock prices had fallen sufficiently so that the 1929 P/E's were well within the range of the P/E's of the 1990s.

The market to book value ratio of the Standard & Poor's industrial stocks trended upward in the 1990s from over three to over four. In 1929 the average ratio was well below four.

In 1995 the Dow Jones Industrial Average increased by 33.5 percent and in 1996 the increase was 26 percent. For the fifteen years ending in 1996 the average had risen by 14.2 percent a year, which beat the 13.4 percent set in 1929 (*New York Times*, January 2, 1997, p. C21). If the stock market in September 1929 was obviously overpriced, then the market in 1997 could also be said to be overpriced. If buying stocks in 1929 was an act of speculation, then buying stocks in the late 1990s is equally speculative.

Obviously, the objective financial measures indicate the market in the mid-1990s has the same degree of optimism as did the 1929 market prior to October 1929. A set of circumstances led to the October crash in 1929, and then real economic events (a major depression) led to further declines. The October 1929 crash and the further price declines did not have to occur.

The raising of the discount rate to 6 percent in August 1929 by the New York Federal Reserve Bank was also separate from Black Thursday (October 24), as were the Hatry collapse and the raising of the interest rate in London since both the later two events occurred in September. But all three events helped set the stage for the crash.

The Snowden orgy of speculation statement and the several regulatory investigations (especially the statements made by the Massachusetts commission) resulted in selling (and price declines) of utility stocks from October 16 to October 24, 1929. Given the many levels of leverage (including holding companies and investment trusts), the effects of the utility stock price declines were multiplied, thus resulting in further selling as margins were called. At some point an overreaction to the price declines set in and a selling panic evolved.

During 1996, stocks rose in value by 26 percent. On Friday, December 6, 1996, the headline (p. 1) of the *Times* (London) was "Greenspan Triggers Worldwide Plunge on Stock Markets." Alan Greenspan, chairman of the U.S. Federal Reserve, issued a warning about the dangers of "irrational exuberance" pushing stock prices too high. In New York, the Dow Jones Industrial Average fell 145 points, but at the close had only fallen 55 points from 6437 to 6382.

Markets in Tokyo, Hong Kong, Paris, Berlin, and London also fell sharply.

During the trading day it was announced that the unemployment rate was 5.4 percent, an increase of 0.2 percent. This indicated that the Federal Reserve would not immediately increase interest rates. Thus, a negative economic factor could be positively interpreted by the market.

THE 1997 MARKET AND ALAN GREENSPAN

The *New York Times*, February 27, 1997, on page one headlined "Greenspan Warns Again That Stocks May Be Too High." He was concerned that many people seemed to think that financial markets had entered a new era of low risk. "But, regrettably, history is strewn with visions of such 'new eras' that in the end have proven to be a mirage."

Unfortunately, Greenspan, the forecaster, cannot be separated from Greenspan, the designer of events. He seems to forget that he can influence what happens to the stock market. He should remember that Adolph Miller and Herbert Hoover got their wish to stop the "orgy of speculation."

On March 25, 1997, the Federal Reserve increased interest rates (federal funds rate) by 25 basis points (from .0500 to .0525). The economy grew at a 5.6 percent rate in the first three months of 1997, and unemployment was reduced to 4.9 percent, the lowest rate in twenty-three years.

While the initial market reaction to Greenspan's efforts to slow the economy and the market was a "sell-off," by May 6, 1997, the Dow hit an all-time high. Thus the "irrational exuberance" statement of Greenspan and the action by the Fed were not enough to dampen long-term the investors' enthusiasm for stocks, given the very healthy economy. In 1929 Snowden's "orgy of speculation" speech was backed up by the change in the utility regulatory climate and an increase in the Bank of England lending rate. In 1997, the Federal Reserve's efforts to reduce the investor's enthusiasm for stock was not reinforced by other economic events. Investors remained bullish.

WHAT WE DO NOT KNOW ABOUT 1929

We do not know as much about the structure of investment trusts in 1929 as we would like. They did own utility stocks and they did use a large amount of leverage, but we do not have exact measures. The market prices of investment trust stocks probably were in excess of asset value, but we do not know by how much.

Another mystery is the amount of investment in stocks by non-U.S. investors and the changes in these investments in October 1929. There were news stories implying a flow of funds from New York to London, but there is no exact measure of the magnitude of the flows.

The dollar-pound exchange rate reflects the withdrawal of investment funds by the British from the United States. The pound went from 4.85\frac{1}{16}$ in January 1929 to 4.88\frac{7}{16}$ maximum price for a pound in October 1929 to 4.87\frac{31}{32}$ in January 1930. While the price change for an English pound is in the expected direction, it is difficult to conjecture the magnitude of the investment liquidation necessary to increase the price of the pound by $.03$\frac{9}{16}$ from January to the middle of October (*Economist*, February 15, 1930, p. 72).

In the fall of 1929 prices of securities in the United Kingdom fell some, but nothing like the severity of the U.S. crash. The *Economist* reported (January 25, 1930, p. 40) that the index of 365 representative securities was 160.8 in October, 147.0 in November, and 147.1 in December. This was a modest drop of 8.5 percent.

The extent of short selling would be of interest. Observers at the scene (e.g., Simmons) thought the magnitude was small compared to the size of the market, but systematic data is not available.

The magnitude of the margin calls and the facts as to whether the response to the calls was supplying further collateral or selling of stock would help us evaluate the impact of margin buying on the level of stock prices.

It is possible to conjecture the cause of price breaks on October 3 and 4 and October 15 to 16, but we cannot give good reasons why the Black Thursday (October 24) and Black Tuesday (October 29) were the days of the largest panic selling. Thus, we have some answers, but there are still areas of ignorance that should be studied.

DIVIDENDS ON STOCK (1929)

For 1928 the *New York Times* (December 31, 1929, p. 28) reported total dividends on common stock of $3.44 billion and for 1929 a total of $4.46 billion, an increase of $1.02 billion or 30 percent. This rate of increase is staggering. In 1928, 221 companies increased their dividends and in 1929, there were 399 companies increasing dividends. The dividends paid in December 1929 ($408 million) were the largest of any month.

It is not surprising that stocks went up in 1929. It is surprising the market crashed.

The financial news focused on the low dividend yields and the extent of speculation rather than the extraordinary growth in dividends. There were good reasons for investing in stocks of U.S. firms in the second half of 1929.

SEVEN THEORIES

The *New York Times* (December 31, 1929, p. 28) listed seven popular theories that prevailed in 1929.

1. There was a new economic era (the year's events had "proven" this false).

2. High money rates were not important to Wall Street (the March crash was attributed to the high call money rate but call money was cheap in October. Also, the October crash occurred significantly after the rate increases by the New York Federal Reserve Bank in August and the Bank of England on September 26).

3. The increase in brokers' loans was caused by new issues (the *Times* believed a more likely cause was "speculation").

4. The 10 times earnings rule for stocks was replaced by 15–25 time earnings (the October crash reaffirmed the rule of 10).

5. The 50–60 percent margins were safe (for the brokers but not for the investors who lost their entire investments).

6. Loans by "others" effectively replaced the loans by banks (the loans by others shrank drastically in October).

7. The Federal Reserve Board attacked the stock market (the *Times* concluded that the efforts of the board prevented an even worse disaster).

SPECULATIVE ORGY OR A NEW ERA

Conventional wisdom is that the first nine months of 1929 were a speculative orgy, but there was also the viewpoint (expressed by academics such as Lawrence, Dice, and Fisher) that there was a new economic era. Events of October 1929 dispelled the illusion that there was a new era where stocks only went up. While the October crash seemed to verify that there had been excessive speculation, my conclusion is somewhat different. With hindsight we know that stock prices on October 1 were higher than they would be again for many years, but it has not been proven that speculation had excessively driven up stock prices in 1929. Aside from the prices of utility stocks and possibly banks, reasonable explanations can be given for the level of stock prices and for the increases in stock prices for the first nine months of 1929.

SOME CONCLUDING OBSERVATIONS

The 1929 market was not obviously overvalued, though pockets (e.g., public utilities) were aggressively valued. Even the level of public utilities stocks could be justified if the regulatory attitudes and processes were not to be changed. But the message that the market was too high (caused by the speculators) was finally accepted by the market in October 1929.

The use of excessive debt leverage is not evil, but it does increase the risk of the investors in stocks. Leverage was widely used in 1929, and when stocks dropped in value the effects of the stock price drops were multiplied by the effects of the debts used by firms, holding companies, investment trusts, and individual investors.

After 1929 the federal government decided that a few select people were to blame for the events of 1929–1933. Not satisfied with merely pointing out the real or imaginary mistakes that were made, unjust criminal charges were brought against Charles Mitchell and Samuel Insull. While both men were judged innocent by juries (one was a directed verdict by the judge), the several defendants in the Mitchell and Insull trials paid the heavy price of being prosecuted by the U.S. government. In many senses this was an attack by the left end of the political spectrum on the "establishment" that anticipated the attack from the right that was to occur in the 1950s from Senator McCarthy. Unfortunately, the attacks in the 1930s hit two men who can be considered to be part of the establishment only because of their personal accomplishments.

The final conclusion is that too often those who have told the 1929 story have merely repeated the tales from nonobjective sources. The people who bought stocks in 1929 (e.g., Irving Fisher) deserve more evenhanded treatment. One did not have to be a speculative fool to have bought stocks in September, October, or November 1929. Unfortunately, the crash that occurred in October 1929 can be replicated in any stock market at any time. But, just as October 1929 did not have to happen, the next crash will also be a surprise and will not be inevitable. We should remember that history repeats itself, but only with surprises.

Bibliography

Balke, N. S., and R. J. Gordon. 1986. Historical data. In *The American business cycle*. Ed. R. J. Gordon. Chicago: University of Chicago Press.

Barsky, R. B. and J. B. DeLong. 1990. Bull and bear markets in the twentieth century. *Journal of Economic History*, (June): 265–68.

Bierman, H., Jr., 1991. *The great myths of 1929 and the lessons to be learned.* Westport, CT: Greenwood Press.

Bluefield Water Works v. P.S.C. 262, U.S. 679 (1923).

Cecchetti, S. G. 1992. Stock market crash of October 1929. In *The new palgrave*. Ed. P. Newman, M. Milgate, and J. Eatwell. London: Macmillan Press.

Committee on Banking and Currency. 1931. *Hearings on performance of the national and federal reserve banking systems.* Washington, D.C.: U.S. Government Printing Office.

———. *Stock Exchange Practices.* 1933. Washington, D.C.: U.S. Government Printing Office.

———. *Stock Exchange Practices.* 1934. Washington, D.C.: U.S. Government Printing Office.

Crisp, J., et al. 1937. *The Hatry case, eight current misconceptions.* London: n.p. (Prepared by seventeen friends of Clarence C. Hatry. Most of the seventeen had impressive credentials.)

DeLong, J. B., and Andrei Schleifer. 1991. The stock market bubble of 1929: Evidence from closed-end mutual funds. *Journal of Economic History*, (September): 675–700.

Federal Power Commission v. Hope Natural Gas Company 320, U.S. 591 (1944).

Fisher, I. 1930. *The stock market crash and after.* New York: Macmillan.

Fisher, Irving Norton. 1956. *My father, Irving Fisher.* New York: Comet.

Friedman, M., and A. J. Schwartz. 1963. *A monetary history of the United States, 1867, 1960.* Princeton: Princeton University Press.

Galbraith, J. K. 1979. The great crash. *Journal of Portfolio Management* (Fall): 60–62.

———. 1961. *The great crash, 1929.* Boston: Houghton Mifflin.

Gordon, R. I. 1986. *The American business cycle.* Chicago: University of Chicago Press.

Hamlin Diary. 1929. Library of Congress, Washington, D.C. (unpublished).

Harrison, G. 1928–1929. *Papers.* New York: Archives of the Federal Reserve Bank of New York (unpublished).

Hatry, C. C. 1939. *Light out of darkness.* Rich and Cowan, Ltd.

Hearing before a Subcommittee of the Committee on Banking and Currency, United States Senate, Part 3. 1931. Washington, D.C.: U.S. Government Printing Office.

Hearings of House Committee on Banking and Currency on Stabilization. April–May 1928.

Hearings of Senate Committee on Banking and Currency on Brokers' Loans. February–March 1928.

Hoover, H. 1952. *The memoirs of Herbert Hoover.* New York: Macmillan.

Investment Bankers Association of America. 1930. *Proceedings of the Nineteenth Annual Convention of the Investment Bankers Association of America.* Chicago.

Jones, F. W. and A. D. Lowe. 1935. Manipulation. In *The security markets.* New York: Twentieth Century Fund.

Kendrick, J. W. 1961. *Productivity trends in the United States.* Princeton: Princeton University Press.

Kindleberger, C. P. 1978. *Manias, panics, and crashes.* New York: Basic Books.

Lawrence, J. S. 1929. *Wall Street and Washington.* Princeton: Princeton University Press.

Liu, T., G. I. Santoni, and C. C. Stone. 1995. In search of stock market babbles: A comment on Rappoport and White. *Journal of Economic History,* (September): 647–54.

Macaulay, F. R. and D. Durand. 1931. *Short selling on the New York Stock Exchange.* New York: Twentieth Century Fund, (mimeographed).

Malkiel, B. G. 1975 and 1996. *A random walk down Wall Street.* New York: Norton.

McDonald, F. 1962. *Insull.* Chicago: University of Chicago Press.

Moggridge, D. 1981. *The collected writings of John Maynard Keynes,* vol xx. London: Macmillan.

Moggridge, D. E. 1992. *Maynard Keynes, an economist's biography.* London: Routledge.

Pecora, F. 1939. *Wall Street under oath.* New York: Simon and Schuster.

Pedersen, J. 1961. Some notes on the economic policy of the United States during the period 1919–1932. In *Money, growth and methodology,* ed. H. Hegeland. Sweden: C.W.K. Gleerup.

Rappoport, P., and E. N. White. 1993. Was there a bubble in the 1929 stock market? *Journal of Economic History,* September, 549–74.

———. 1944. Was the crash of 1929 expected? *American Economic Review* (March): 271–81.

Samuelson, P. A. 1979. Myths and realities about the crash and depression. *Journal of Portfolio Management* (fall).

Santoni, G. J. 1987. The great bull markets 1924–29 and 1982–87: Speculative bubbles or economic fundamentals? *Federal Reserve Bank of St. Louis Review,* (November): 16–29.

Schwed, F., Jr. 1940. *Where are the customers' yachts?* New York: Simon and Schuster.

Shachtman, T. 1979. *The day America crashed.* New York: Putnam.

Simmons, E. H. H. 1930. *The principal causes of the stock market crisis of nineteen twenty-nine.* Philadelphia: Transportation Club.

Sirkin, G. 1975. The stock market of 1929 revisited: A note. *Business History Review* (summer): 223–231.

Sloan, A. P., Jr. 1963. *My years with General Motors.* Garden City, NY: Doubleday.

Sobel, R. 1968. *The great bull market, Wall Street in the 1920s.* New York: Norton.

———. 1968. *Panic on Wall Street.* New York: Macmillan.

Stock Market Study. Hearings before the Committee on Banking and Currency, U.S. Senate. Washington, D.C.: U.S. Government Printing Office, 1955.

Thomas, G., and M. Morgan-Witts. 1979. *The day the bubble burst.* Garden City, NY: Doubleday and Company, Inc.

U.S. Senate, Subcommittee of the Committee on Banking and Currency. *Stock Exchange Practices Hearings.* Washington, D.C.: U.S. Government Printing Office, 1933.

Wanniski, J. 1987. The Smoot-Hawley tariff and the stock market crash of 1929. *Midland Corporate Finance Journal* (summer): 6–23.

White, E. N. 1995. Stock market bubbles? A reply. *Journal of Economic History,* (September): 655–65.

Wigmore, B. A. 1985. *The crash and its aftermath: A history of securities markets in the United States, 1929–33.* Westport, CT: Greenwood.

NEWSPAPERS AND OTHER PERIODICALS

The Boston Daily Globe, October 1929.
The Commercial and Financial Chronicle, October 1929.
The Economist, 1929, 1930.
The Federal Reserve Bulletin.
The Financial Times, September 1929–January 1930.
The First National City Bank of New York Newsletter, 1929–1930.
Forbes, October 15, 1925.
The Listener, 1929, London.
The Magazine of Wall Street, 1929.
The New York Herald Tribune, September 6, 1929.
The New York Times, 1929 and 1930.
The Wall Street Journal, October 1929.
The Washington Post, October 1929.

Index

About the Author

HAROLD BIERMAN, JR. is the Nicholas H. Noyes Professor of Business Administration at the Johnson Graduate School of Management, Cornell University. He is the author of several books, including *The Great Myths of 1929 and the Lessons to Be Learned* (Greenwood, 1991).

ISBN 0-313-30629-X

EAN

9 780313 306297

HARDCOVER BAR CODE

90000>